"COVER TO COVER"

EVERYONE HAS A STORY.
THIS IS ANNIE'S -
FROM COVER UP TO COVER UP

BY:

CHRISTINE THIEL

CONTENTS

PREFACE

Cover To Cover is a biography, told by Annie. Nothing in Annie's life was as it seemed.

I wrote this book to free my mind. In fact, it's my autobiography.

Who am I? I'm a middle-aged woman who has used life's experiences to develop my character.

Cover To Cover's story is about my life and how I survived and grew. It exposes the deceit created by adults and continued to follow me, and later, haunting me through my childhood and adult life.

Everyone has their own story, and it may be as interesting, or more interesting than Annie's. It's what I have done with my story which makes it stand out in its own right, and makes it an interesting, readable book. There will be tears, but there will also be laughs, and a feeling of victory and achievement from "Cover To Cover".

I made the decision to publish my story to demonstrate we can survive everything life throws at us, and we can grow stronger because of, or in spite of it.

Books have been written about personal growth, based on life's experiences. They become "self-help" books. This is not a self-help book.

Cover To Cover demonstrates the blessings and blows in my life. How the untimely deaths of my young mother, and later my grandmother, shaped my childhood and adolescence. At these strategic stages in my life, decisions were made for me by well-meaning or controlling adults, without asking me how I was feeling or explaining their decisions. In fact they barely acknowledged me, while making all the decisions about my life. In my early years I withdrew and resigned my fate to the decision makers. This withdrawal did not help me when I entered adulthood.

What can readers learn from Annie's story?

I am demonstrating there is an "up" side to life no matter how bleak it may have seemed at the time. I'd spent my early life pleasing everyone to avoid punishment or demoralization.

I grew from a submissive "quiet little thing", into a self-confident, independent, decisive individual, but not without some ill effects. The lessons along the way helped me to define my priorities - to confront and change the things I could, and to let go of the things I couldn't. I learned to focus on what mattered.

I have developed a happy knack of laughing at the ridiculous and ironic, and seeing the positive and happy side of most things, when it's appropriate. It's my intention to convey the "happy knack".

The story begins at a time in my life when I could reflect on all the events that made me the person I am - stronger, more independent, self-reliant, and much, much wiser.

Each chapter stands alone as a story in its own right. When the chapters are linked, a much bigger, clearer picture evolves. I believe the story demonstrates my mature confidence and vitality, and how I came to be this way.

I am curious, imaginative, resilient, and pursue activities that improve my life. utilising my capabilities. This has helped me to analyse each episode and deal with it in a practical way.

I am optimistic and see the world as a positive place of adventure. I used first-hand experiences when I embarked on this project.

I am realistic and live in the here and now, strongly defending myself, my lifestyle and my survival, based on my early life experiences.

I genuinely respect home, family, work and community, and am conscientious and dependable. This respect is reflected particularly in chapter fifteen, Tough Love, and other related sections of the book.

I generally enjoy life and have a cheeky sense of humor. As I travel around this country with my caravan and four wheel drive I see things and meet people which give me the means by which I can develop my wit. Observing peoples' personalities and characters give me all the entertainment I need to help my literary efforts flourish.

Cover to Cover reveals a vivid picture of my life's experiences, and what can be positively achieved with courage, perseverance and persistence.

OVERVIEW

Cover To Cover is a biography, told by Annie.

Nothing in Annie's life was as it seemed.

Everyone has sad and happy time during in their lives.

Books have also been written about personal growth, based on life's experiences. They become self-help books. This is not a self-help book.

What can you learn from Annie's story?

Only by reading Cover to Cover will you gain a vivid picture of the experiences, and the outcome.

The author has a happy knack of seeing the positive and happy side of most things, when it's appropriate.

You will relate to Annie's life and become her friend in Cover To Cover.

INTRODUCTION

How much do we know about our genetic origins? Annie knew nothing about her personal history until she was in her mid-life, when she learned no one had told her the truth.

This is a true story, as told by the woman who is featured in the story.

Once you have opened this book and read the first paragraph, you will want to keep reading to the very end.

You will want to share Annie's experiences and you will want to learn how she coped and overcame to move on and live a full and interesting life. Sometimes, you will be brought to tears as you feel what she felt.

You will laugh to tears as you admire her attitude to adversity and the impact it had on her once the cover-up was uncovered.

Everyone has had some of Annie's experiences. It's how she faced them and overcame them which makes her unique and will keep you reading.

No one knows what plans are in place for their life. How we confront life determines how we use adversity and its consequences – whether we survive and grow or crumble.

Annie had her turn at crumbling but she grew to be a strong, resilient woman, mother and grandmother. She did most of it alone, without the support of parents, family or spouse.

Annie was a single entity who never felt unconditional love and support. She survived to tell her tale.

CHAPTER 1

LIFE BEGAN AT FOURTEEN

On the day of her fourteenth birthday, Annie's dad destroyed everything she had been raised to believe about her family, with just four words.

"I'm not your father", he announced, like he was declaring some sort of victory.

Those four words frightened her, but Annie didn't know how she was supposed to feel.

The man she knew and loved as her father seemed to take delight in making this life-shattering announcement with no regard for its effect on her.

Annie's dad had come to spend her birthday at her grandparent's house.

He entered the house with the usual supply of alcohol – three "king browns" of beer, and a flagon of claret. After the obligatory greeting with Annie's grandmother, he summoned Anna, "Come out to the car, I want to talk to you".

Her grandmother had a cold look on her face but said nothing.

Annie thought it was a bit unusual, but being the obedient "little girl", she followed him out to his little car parked in the backyard.

When she was settled in the front passenger seat, he began by asking, "Do you know about the birds and the bees?"

"Yes", she answered, thinking she knew it all from her high school mother craft classes and the smutty jokes she heard on the school bus. She put two and two together, but realised she really had no actual experience.

That's when he made the monumental announcement. "I'm not your bilogical father."

Annie didn't know how to react. She didn't know how she was supposed to feel. Should she be shocked? Should she be disgusted? Should she be hurt and disappointed?

The emotion she really experienced was confusion. She was more confused now than she had ever been before, even more than when her mother died.

When the full story was revealed Annie realised her life had been a cover up - a tragic cover up of several moral dilemmas.

Annie had hidden her emotions most of her life because no one ever seemed to be interested in how she felt. She had always been told what to do, and to stay out of the way.

Her heart broke with the shocking announcement, but she was afraid to show emotion in case she was punished for disrespecting.

Annie had always known this man as her dad, but he changed her life forever, with a most bitter, heartless declaration.

Oblivious to her feelings he went on, "And I'm sending you to boarding school next year, to get you away from your grandmother's clutches."

Annie was niaive and innocent, but this was something else. She felt shocked at this announcement. How was she going to deal with this new information? What was her role to be in all this? She had no say in any of it.

"What was wrong with her grandparents?" she wondered. *"What had they done to make him take her away from them?"*

"Why was her father so bitter toward them?" Annie wondered. Why was he using her to spite them?

They were the only family she knew, and she only knew their way of life. Annie was most certainly not prepared for boarding school. She was only halfway through the second year of high school.

She dared not ask these questions out loud. At fourteen she understood none of this.

Her dad said her mother had an affair with a married man. He didn't disclose his name, but hinted at who it may have been.

This little detail was clarified more than seventy- years later.

Annie became the first born of an arranged marriage of the couple she knew as her parents.

nnie believed the marriage was arranged to hide the fact her unmarried mother was expecting the child of a married man, and to cover up the prospective husband's suspected homosexuality.

The image of her dead mother, and the relationship with the grandparents who raised her for the previous eight years, was shattered.

Until the 1970's, it was illegal to be sexually alternate in this state. Homosexuals were considered to be criminals. The community also feared homosexuals, and there were numerous incidents of "poofter bashing".

This marriage began on very shaky ground.

"What the hell was boarding school all about?" she wondered through the haze of all this new information.

She had only just settled into high school, and now she had to leave her friends and start at a new school – a school she had never heard of.

Her dad had enrolled Annie in the college affiliated with the church he attended, while her grandparent's church was affiliated with another college.

The act of enrolling Annie in the College he supported, was to show the world he had paid for the education, and not the wealthy, influential grandparents. He also clarified to her that he had borrowed the money to pay for it. She guessed he told her to demonstrate the sacrifices he was making to get her away from the only family she knew.

Was she supposed to feel grateful or obliged, or both?

About fifty years later Annie felt disgust when she realised his intentions were to use her to spite and hurt the mother of his dead wife - the woman who was his mother-in-law, the grandmother of his child. The woman who probably saved him from going to prison for his sexuality, and who was raising one of his children. This woman was now "the enemy".

11

Now he wanted to claim the credit for his daughter's education, by enrolling her in an expensive boarding school.

When all this became apparent to her, Annie's only reaction to his deeds was, *"What a hypocrite!"*

At the time, Annie was shocked but resigned to believe the decision was made. She had to dutifully comply, as usual. This was the way things were done.

Once again, no one asked her how she felt about any of it. She was expected to take in all this new information, to swallow hard, and get on with it. God only knows how her grandmother felt.

While still coming to terms with the idea of leaving the only home she knew to do something completely alien to her, Annie had to deal with another heartbreak.

It was December of the same year when her grandmother had minor surgery. Annie was sent to stay with a great Aunty, her grandmother's sister. She continued her daily routine of attending school during the week and attending Church studies on Saturday morning. After about two weeks her grandmother was released from hospital and stayed with her eldest son and his wife at their farm.

Her grandmother had been out for only a few days when complications returned her to hospital. Three days later Annie was told, "Nana died".

Once again, another chapter of her life had been closed and she'd have to start again.

Annie only had vague memories of the week leading up to the funeral. Her memories of the graveside were much more vivid.

She sobbed aloud and uncontrollably. Something was holding her back from letting the small posy of flowers drop from her hand onto the coffin at the bottom of the grave. Annie never knew why she felt such panic and distress.

Was she afraid to get too close to the edge of the grave? Was she afraid to make the final gesture of goodbye, or was she still afraid of her Nanna?

Many years later she tried to analyse her recollection of the graveside experience. She knew it wasn't a terror type of fear, but perhaps it was the fear of doing the wrong thing, and being punished again, for something she couldn't control.

Once again, she was reprimanded by an adult for bad behaviour that she didn't comprehend. Again, no one asked her how she felt. Annie just had to do as she was told, but she never understood why.

Someone, she didn't know who, was pushing her closer to the edge of the grave, shaking her arm and the hand which held the posy. Annie was afraid of heights but managed to look down into the dark depths of the grave. The flowers fell on to the coffin, without her deliberate gesture of offering them in a final act of love and respect.

Then it was all over and her life went on in a blur. She couldn't even remember where she lived or who took care of her in the ensuing weeks.

The following Sunday Annie was to be confirmed into the Church. Her grandmother had designed the beautiful white dress she was to wear to this very significant Christian occasion. Someone had taken Annie's completed dress to the hospital so her grandmother could see it finished. Her grandmother never saw her own dress, which she had also designed.

This very special day of Annie's life was just a haze.

Instead of it being an occasion to celebrate, it was a sad day for all the family. No one ever considered Annie's feelings about any of it. She just went through the motions of the ceremony as she had rehearsed it. She was a good girl as long as she had it all right on the day. She had to keep up the family's image to the Church community. She didn't want to embarrass anyone.

It was Christmas school holidays, the end of her life with the family she had grown to know over the previous eight years. Annie was packed up and relocated to a family her dad knew, about one hundred kilometres away. They were a loving, hard-working, Christian family. No one mentioned her Nanna again.

The next few weeks of the holidays were spent shopping for the College uniform, and sewing name tags on every item of clothing - the dresses, shirts, blazer, jumper, school tie, underwear, and sox and shoes.

It had been a hard year for Annie since the day of her fourteenth birthday in June. She had to deal with the news the man she knew as her father wasn't. She had to make adjustments and prepare herself for changing school, and moving away from the home and the people she knew as family. Now she was also dealing with the sudden death of her grandmother.

She didn't understand why her dad kept raising the fact he wasn't included in her grandmother's will. Annie wasn't a beneficiary either. Someone else in the family even took her grand mother's collection of beautiful jewellery.

Her dad used to say, "She didn't even leave me a chair."

Annie knew he was very bitter, and in hindsight may have been justified, considering the sacrifice he made. However, he seemed to forget his mother-in-law also covered his illegal sexuality with the arranged marriage.

Annie concluded there wasn't much respect between them and that her sister was the only connection she had left with her close family.

Now it was time for Annie to focus on her next new life step.

She was as ready for college admission day as she could be, but she was not prepared for boarding school.

CHAPTER 2

GROWING UP

Annie was lost. At fourteen she was still a child, and not prepared for this new stage of her life on her own.

No one had prepared her for any of her new experiences. None of her family had been to boarding school before her. There was no one she could ask about what she should expect.

Annie was simply not prepared – not even to manage her personal hygiene. Her grandmother had taken care of these things for Annie until she died, six months after Annie's dad told her about her beginnings.

In fact, it was family practice to have a bath on Saturday whether they needed it or not. They all had to be clean for church on Sunday.

On the other days of the week, they just wash their face, hands and feet. Maybe the other women in the household washed more of themselves, but Annie wasn't taught this.

Saving rainwater was the object of these water conservation practices, but Annie wasn't sure how they all lived so close in the same house.

Her first menstrual period at boarding school was an absolute disgrace. Annie was too embarrassed to change herself. She didn't know about the sanitary furnaces in the bathrooms. She didn't even know how to wash blood-soaked clothing. Annie's grandmother had protected her and done all this, but she was gone, and this was a whole new outside world.

Annie believed her grandmother meant well but didn't prepare her for life on her own. Her dad certainly wasn't any help.

A thoughtful, understanding teacher helped Annie clean herself up, and showed her how to deal with this facet of personal hygiene. Annie saw the other girls showering daily and she followed their example.

"I must have been an absolute joy to share the dorm with," she reflected. "Eeew!"

For Annie the whole time was just a blur, well, all except for this disgusting experience. She felt ashamed and depressed.

Annie had to adapt to sharing a dormitory with five other girls, one of whom was a prefect – a senior student elected to be a leader and role model.

Annie had been raised as an only child, and always had her own bed and room.

Tina had been taught to respect authority. She was terrified of anyone older or in a position of authority. The prefect was a friendly leader who helped Annie to relax and settle in. Roommates guided her. Annie's own observations were the best life lessons. She had difficulty connecting to people here, so she kept her distance and spent much time alone in the dormitory or common room.

At the beginning of the first term Annie auditioned for the college choir and was selected to be in the soprano section. After all her recent events, she still retained her love of music, especially singing. She was very proud to be chosen but no one in her family acknowledged her achievement. She didn't ever know if they were aware of her skills, or if they cared.

Annie took her chance at athletics and sport trials. She loved sprinting and played a goal shooter in Netball.

She was adjusting to new subject choices and new people and boarding away from anything she had known as home.

She was in third year secondary. It was vital in this era to pass this level to decide on any future employment or career. Annie had no ambition, nor any plans for her future. She had never been encouraged to pursue any career direction. In fact, apart from housework for her grandmother, Annie didn't know what work life there was outside of the farm.

Prompted by her dad's belief and suspicion, Annie believed she was being "trained" to keep house for her aging grandparents. This would never be fulfilled.

Perhaps this was what her dad was alluding to when he declared he was getting Annie away from her grandmother's "clutches".

Only a few months after her grandmother's death, in spite of her dad, Annie's life was being "managed" by her tyrannical, controlling aunty.

The first school holidays were spent having her crooked, decayed teeth extracted and replaced by a partial denture. Annie never knew who had paid the dental bill, but she assumed her aunt had. This aunty made appointments at the dentist and chiropractor.

The first school holidays were spent having her crooked, decayed top front teeth extracted and replaced by a partial denture. Annie never knew who had paid the dental bill but assumed her aunt had. Her aunty also made appointments with the chiropractor to relieve her back pain. She never heard about these things from her dad.

Annie had often complained of back ache since she was nine years old. No one seemed to take an interest other than to console her with, "You'll be alright. It's only growing pains."

So, under this assumption, nothing was done to investigate Annie's pain until this Aunty took matters into her own hands. Annie never knew if she was supposed to be grateful and obliged. She also never really knew if the treatment made any improvements to her back condition.

Forty years later, she had surgery for "growing pains".

Annie had to concentrate on passing all the new subjects at this new school. The only subjects she carried over from her last school were English, Maths and typing. Some of her new subjects were similar to the former school, but there were vast differences in content and teaching methods.

Annie spent the entire year adapting and learning in a haze. She became sick during the year. She woke one Sunday morning feeling unwell, but there was nothing specifically wrong with her.

Her dad visited her on the Sunday and they spent time chatting. No mention was made of her health.

After two days in sick bay she was sent back to the classroom. The school work didn't get any easier.

Many years later Annie later concluded she had probably suffered some form of mental break down at the time.

Still no one, other than College staff asked her how she felt, or what she was feeling, and the haze continued.

Her dad would visit her about every second weekend between weekends at home. They'd go for drives and use the time for Annie to practice her driving on her Learner's Permit. He'd fall asleep in the passenger seat leaving the instructions, "Stay away from taxis and buses."

She believed her feelings didn't count to anyone who mattered to her. She failed all her subjects except Geography. But she didn't fail her spare class.

Annie didn't have a full curriculum, so the spare lesson time was spent in a classroom allocated to any students who had spare classes, where they studied or completed assignments.

Annie shared a desk with a tall, nice, senior student, who was also a prefect. They became very close and a relationship developed. They'd sneak out at night to spend time together in private. Spending time together - just talking, cuddling and kissing.

Annie's heart was broken when he broke off their relationship after leaving college the following year to pursue further education at a tertiary institution. He had a different lifestyle with different priorities, and she was no longer one of them.

After Annie recovered, she could still look back and cherish the memories of the time spent with this very nice man. One of her better experiences to this point in her life.

Her father had arranged for her to attend a second year at boarding school, to repeat the year she had failed. He took great delight in reminding her of the sacrifices he made to borrow the money to send her to college for the second year. Was she supposed to feel guilty or obliged?

History was her most difficult subject. She couldn't relate to all those dates and places.

Annie loved Geography as it was relevant and happening all around, English, except Shakespeare, was right up her alley. Annie loved writing. Art was pointless. She couldn't even draw a recognizable stick figure. The graphic lettering the teacher took great pains to teach became redundant with her job choices, and later, with the invention of computers.

Basic Arithmetic was simple enough, but Annie never understood Algebra. Simple Geometry made more sense to her as she grew older than she did in school.

Typing was easy for Annie. She had an idea she would probably need it in future employment, so she applied herself to this subject.

Annie's History teacher spent hours of her out of class time to tutor her. The teacher's efforts were rewarded when she passed this, and all the other subjects, at her second attempt.

A school counselor recommended that Annie leave school, based on her struggle to achieve academic success. She was discouraged from returning for another year of secondary education. If truth be told, Annie's dad probably couldn't borrow anymore money to pay for another year at College.

Annie was secretly relieved.

Boarding school turned out to be a better experience than Annie had expected. She made friends, went on excursions with her classes. The college choir performed at churches and theatres around the city and nearby country towns. She felt very proud to represent the College doing something she really enjoyed.

Then it was time for Annie to move in with her dad. It had been more than ten years since she lived with him. From childhood to adolescence – he was a virtual stranger to her.

CHAPTER 3

HOME LIFE

Annie was left to ponder.

How did her mother die - the actual cause of death and not just the "clinical" reason stated on the Death Certificate.

Why did her mother have another man's child if her parents were happily married?

"If mum was initially pregnant to someone other than the man I knew as dad, why didn't she marry him?" Tina pondered.

"What sort of life was it for both of them?"

"Mum was bound into a sham relationship," she reasoned, *"and dad went along with it, perhaps hoping there would be something in it for him eventually – reward for his sacrifice, from his wealthy in-laws, for his role in the social cover-up."*

Annie's dad still lived his life how he pleased, with little consideration for his wife and child at home. He'd work all day, then stay in the pub until closing time, while her mother was on her own – a normal woman, happy and kind, raising a child on her own. She was known as a loving, healthy person, married to a man who was not her husband in the biblical sense. Tied, yet not able to lead a normal, happy, married life at home. It was all a false facade.

Annie concluded her mother went outside the marriage to seek closeness and love, which resulted in two more pregnancies.

"What a sad, lonely life," Annie reflected.

Her Dad wasn't always the happy-go-lucky social and generous bloke his friends and family knew him to be.

"He didn't treat me very well," Annie recalled. *"He abused and accused, and was physically violent to me"*. She knew him to be a suspicious, spiteful, controlling bully.

He often referred to his mother-in-law as a controlling person. He was even resentful toward his late wife, and passed the guilt on to Annie.

Right until the day before he died, he accused Annie of concealing her mother's affairs.

Annie told him she had no recollection of ever seeing anyone other than her dad and their friends at their house.

What a way for him to go through life! Holding grudges and bitterness, and blaming Annie for concealing what he believed she knew.

Even when she denied any knowledge of the alleged affair, he accused Annie of lying about it. He wouldn't accept her recollection of the time. What could she say?

He asked about a lot of the memories of a four-year-old child. What would a young child know of these things, and what could she remember more than fifty years later?

She was shocked by the insinuation, implying she knew of her mother's affairs. Annie was very hurt when he kept accusing her of lying about it.

If her dad came back from the dead for a day, she'd let him have some truths with both barrels. She'd let him know how distressed she was when he physically punished her for his belief she had been peeping in the window at the boarder, no matter how much she denied it or defended herself. She'd also remind him of the fact he preferred the pub to home.

Annie felt her mother must have wanted to be loved and cuddled, just as she herself needed to be loved and cuddled.

Her mother was married with two kids sixteen months apart, the youngest was severely handicapped. She worked hard around the house and milked the cow. Even her family and friends confirmed she was house-proud, at least until a few weeks before her death.

Annie recalled her family never seemed to have much. They lived in a very basic fibro-cement cottage without running water, hot or cold, or any other mod cons. She remembered the outside toilet down the back yard.

They drove around in draughty old cars.

Annie's parents had known each other as friends since their teen years. They went to local dances with their friends. They both loved music and they both loved to dance.

Annie's mother was pregnant to a married man who had a family of his own.

Annie felt her mother must have been living in this lonely, love-less marriage, in the humble cottage, which was almost a marital prison. Only a certain amount of freedom, but not free.

These recollections brought Annie to remember a situation earlier in her own life. She was eighteen, pregnant and unmarried. The child's father didn't want the responsibility.

Had Annie married her Dad at eighteen years of age, as he proposed, she would have been bound morally in an awful situation. What life would it have been? Not truly married, not able to meet a nice young man, especially with a child in the picture. What lengths was this man prepared to go to protect his sexuality?

"What a dreadful concept!" Annie shuddered at the thought.

She now wondered if it would have been legal. Even if he wasn't her biological father, the law and community considered him to be her father as stated on her Birth Certificate, would it have been legal? Or would it be considered incest, and therefore illegal? Who would have allowed such an arrangement under those circumstances?

Annie's mother was bound in such a situation - Married to a homosexual friend, with a child, but no closeness or support. She believed he loved her mother, but only as a very close friend.

Then, her mother became pregnant again, seven months after the birth of her eldest daughter. The child was born mentally and physically disabled. Another burden to add to her mother's already overloaded emotions. The poor young woman!

Or was she just an ungrateful flighty woman?

Annie's mother must have been living in absolute turmoil. She could almost feel the misery her mother might have felt.

Annie wondered if her mother loved the fathers of her babies. What about the father of her second child, and the third child she was carrying at the time of her death?

What an awful chain of events! The disastrous assortment of relationships, the cover up, and the consequences, which lead to the premature death of this twenty-five-year-old, pregnant mother of two. Tragic!

Annie's grandmother felt the loss with more intensity than other members of the family. Was it because she now felt remorse for her cover-up,the arranged marriage had created?

This was the first major change to Annie's life. She was four years old. Her sister was three.

She recalled she was never really considered or involved in any of these events, especially the death of her mother and the funeral.

While her mother was being buried, Annie was sent to play with friends. It seemed everyone else grieved at the death of this young woman, but Annie's feelings were never considered.

"Children should be seen and not heard," The adults in the family would repeat, over and over again – often.

She didn't recall when, or who explained her mother had died.

After it was all over, Annie and her sister were taken back to their little humble cottage by their Dad.   He employed housekeepers to look after the two girls and the house.

Their dad still stayed at the pub until closing time, which at the time was six o'clock, rather than going home to his little girls, and to support the housekeeper.

The young housekeepers had to cope with it all, and keep his meal until he came home.

Even several years later, after Annie left boarding school and lived with him, he expected her to be the housekeeper, to cook his meals, water his precious vegetable garden, to wash his filthy work clothes and his car. Meanwhile he continued his lifestyle, staying at the hotel until closing time, ten o'clock, showing her no consideration, support, or love.

Adnnie remembered him for his controlling and bullying. *"He was a selfish, controlling, spiteful, sexually alternate man,"* she concluded.

CHAPTER 4

LIFE PLAN

As Annie went through life, she was convinced peoples' lives were planned long before they were born. Whether they were Christian, believed in creation, the universe or evolution, she was convinced there was a life plan for everyone.

As people encountered good and bad experiences at every age, their characters developed.

She believed people either became survivors or victims. They became stronger or crumbled under the pressure. Sometimes they completely withdrew from society.

The skills attained during life made people very resourceful and independent, or they became weak and bitter because there were high expectations of them for which they were not prepared.

Their experiences may have also been too hard to handle and caused emotional and psychological collapse.

People encountered birth and death, happiness and sadness, joy, trauma and tragedy.

Personalities were developed by facing the issues and managing them.

Someone once wrote, "A man (or woman) who is true to themselves, in the interest of all men, will always have enemies, but among the genuine, they will never lack friends".

Annie believed some people became dependent and relied on someone else to deal with everything that confronted them. They never gained enough inner and physical strength to deal with anything beyond the norm. The onus was then on the strong one to deal with the problem, while the weak one was relieved of any stresses and expectations.

The strong, independent person assessed the issue, developed a strategy to confront it and then dealt with it, sometimes in stages, but they ultimately dealt with it, no matter how long it took.

Annie's mother's death, when she was four, set the scene for life changes, which included adapting to the different lifestyles of the families she lived with.

She was also separated from her handicapped sister who was sixteen months younger than her. It just happened, and life went on.

Annie's grandparents regularly took her to visit her disabled sister until her grandmother died. Yet again Annie's routine was broken and the regular visits stopped.

Learning her dad wasn't her father on the day she turned fourteen, and her grandmother's sudden death six months later, drastically changed her life once more.

She had to close the door on an episode to begin a new life all over again, and life went on.

CHAPTER 5

PRIMARY MOVE

Annie began school at the local primary school when she turned six. A housekeeper her dad employed still cared for her and her sister at their dad's home.

After the first year, he gave up trying to retain reliable housekeepers. He took her to her grandparent's farm fifty miles away, and left her to live with them. After much discussion with them, her younger sister was admitted into an institution for dependent mental health patients. She spent the rest of her life in a number of institutions and group homes.

So Annie had to start a new life, in a new family, at a new home and school, without her sister and her dad, and far from the home she knew. Annie had visited the farm before with her mum and dad many times. This time it was permanent.

Annie's grandparents, her two uncles and their families lived at the farm. They were her mother's parents and two brothers, their wives and her cousins. This was Annie's new home. An entirely alien lifestyle.

In this environment, Annie learned that beer and soft drinks were for birthdays and Christmas, unlike her dad, who drank beer and wine every day.

The family entertained relatives or friends with Sunday lunch, usually roast chicken fresh from the chook shed.

Annie's grandfather enjoyed a small port every night before tea. He would also pour a glass for her grandmother and a tiny sip for Annie. This was not her first introduction to the etiquette of port drinking.

While still living at her dad's house she sometimes stayed with the farming family across the road. It was here she was initiated to the port-drinking "club". In this wine growing district, customers traditionally went to the winery cellar door to fill stone jars of varying capacity, with the tipple of choice. Annie's neighbour would tip up the jar and pour a small amount into a small enamel cup to share with the neighbour she called "uncle".

He was a kind man who used to take Annie on his faithful, old horse to round up the sheep.

She had left all these things behind and they became happy memories. She did return to the farm during school holidays on two more occasions.

Now, in her new home, she had to learn to adapt to the new family and lifestyle. Church on Sundays, religious festivals, and religious studies were her grandmother's laws.

Her siblings were her first cousins. The girl was five months older, and the two boys were six years younger.

The two girls attended the same high school, but took different buses, were in different classes, and had different friends. In fact they were totally different in character, interests and hobbies.

Annie was an average student, while her cousin was more successful academically and socially.

Her cousin would want to play dress ups with makeup, while Annie preferred to play with the animals, her bike and her two younger male cousins outside, around the yard and in the sand pit, with toy trucks and tractors.

They both played Netball, and spent time training together at home. They loved throwing goals, sometimes one hundred a day. Annie was a good goalie.

Forty years later Annie's female cousin admitted she didn't like her very much as they grew up, and she had tried to manipulate circumstances so Annie didn't attend the same high school. It didn't work, and they were never in the same class. At this time, the new information had minimal impact.

Annie's grandparents moved to the new house on the hill - high on a hill that overlooked almost the entire farm- and the original homestead where one of Annie's uncles and his family then lived.

Her dad used to visit occasionally on a Sunday, with beer and wine in hand, and his ever-present cigarettes. Annie wasn't allowed to hang around. She'd greet him with great excitement when he arrived, but then she had to go away and play, while the adults talked. The words *"Children should be seen and not heard"*, kept echoing through her mind.

Annie loved running, singing and listening to music. She was in the school choir and played in the primary school band, but no-one seemed to care.

Nobody ever seemed to notice her or her skills, or her interests. When she expressed an interest in learning to play the piano, they sold it. The excuse was, it wouldn't fit into the new house and no one played it anymore.

Annie believed they really didn't want to pay for lessons. Or perhaps the piano reminded her grandparents of their daughter, because they always said it was hers. Annie had never heard her mother play, but her dad loved playing music and singing.

However they always noticed when she had done wrong or when she was disobedient. No one gave her the benefit of the doubt, or asked her what she'd done, or why. The stick would come out in the hands of her nanna, and Annie would be hit four or five times, usually across the back and legs, for being a "naughty girl".

She cried a lot in private when no one was around.

As long as Annie was obedient, "seen and not heard", "spoke when she was spoken to", and "respected her elders", she was safe.

Why couldn't they treat her as they would have liked to be treated? Maybe how they treated her mother?

She became more confused at her new primary school. Twin girls in the upper school tormented and bullied Annie every day because she was different. She didn't know how or why, but suspected the two girls may have known more about her family circumstances than she did. The girls used to say, "You don't have a mummy!"

The tormenting took its toll on her health, and occasionally, for no obvious reason, Annie would vomit in the morning, giving her a day off from school, and away from the bullying. She eventually told her grandmother about the teasing and this time she believed her. Her nanna visited the twins' parents, but the bullying continued, even intensified, until they left the school.

When Annie's grandmother was angry with her, she would say, "You're enough to make a parson swear!" How bad and disobedient could she have been?

When her much loved Grandfather "taught" her how the male reproductive organs worked, she was sworn to secrecy and never said a word to anyone. At the age of twelve Annie did experience what happened when a man became sexually aroused – often.

Adults were not considered to be abusive, or violent, and abusive relationships were private and never discussed outside the home.

Discipline was not considered to be abuse. "Spare the rod, spoil the child" was the motto of the day.

CHAPTER 6

SEEN AND NOT HEARD

Only a few weeks after Annie left boarding school and moved in to her dad's house, she began clerical work at a local industry, not far from where she lived.

One afternoon her dad arrived home from work one Friday evening, then reversed out of the driveway and quickly drove up the road. Annie had no idea where he was going, but it wasn't unusual. They didn't talk about anything much.

He returned home and announced she would begin a new job on Monday, but she had to wait in the driveway for someone to pick her up on Monday morning. Annie had no idea who would pick her up and what the job would be.

She also had to do the house keeping for her dad. Cooking, cleaning, washing and watering the garden. She tried to grow some flowers to brighten up her surroundings around the two bedroom, fibro cottage.

Annie liked to play sport and her boyfriend also played sport. To be ready to go with him to his game on Saturdays, she had to do the washing very early in the morning.

She had to light the copper for hot water, often with wet wood, and bucket the water from the rainwater tank to the copper. When the water was hot she'd bucket it to the washing machine, do all the washing, including her dad's filthy work clothes. No matter how much she had to do, she was always ready to go out when her boyfriend arrived.

He was a genuine, honest Christian man, two years older than Annie. He played Australian Rules Football at the highest level in the State. We spent a lot of time at "Footy" and spending time with his friends in his home town. He was very popular, and I thought I really loved him, and at the time I probably did.

Annie's dad came home every night after the pub closed. He'd often bring people home and they'd party to the wee hours of the morning. He would then go to work a few hours later, to drive a semi-trailer for the full day of work. There were no random breath tests in those days.

Meanwhile, Annie was becoming exhausted and miserable. She couldn't get a sound night's sleep because the party noise penetrated the thin walls. She didn't have any rights in his home. Most of the visitors her dad brought to the house didn't even know she was trying to sleep in the next room. Her dad didn't show her any consideration or respect.

Annie would go to work tired and angry. She had no one to share her feelings with. She certainly couldn't talk to her dad. She sometimes told her boyfriend, but he couldn't help.

Everything she did was not good enough for her dad. He always seemed to be yelling at her. He never spent the time to show her how he wanted things done. Even though she was still learning to cook, he never had the courtesy to be home for the evening meal she had proudly prepared.

He probably related Annie's ways to her grandmother's ways, and he seemed to display his resentment toward her. The bitterness continued.

She didn't have any nearby friends, no hobbies, no television, so she spent many hours alone, listening to the radio. Her dad was rarely home by the time she went to bed.

Her boyfriend wasn't allowed to visit during the week. His family didn't have the telephone, so to phone him in an emergency she had to phone his neighbours.

Annie's dad brought a boarder home - a Kiwi bloke whose car had broken down. The boarder stayed a few months, sharing her dad's room because there were no other spare rooms in the little cottage.

Not long after the boarder had moved in, her dad accused her of peeping through his bedroom window.

Annie didn't even know where the accusation came from; no matter how much she denied it, he had made up his mind. Annie had no right of defense. A simple "no" didn't do it, and he never gave her the benefit of the doubt. Annie cried in fear, and the disappointment her dad accused her of this, and he didn't believe her when she denied it.

In fact, his accusations intensified into rage, and the more she denied them, the angrier he became. Then he started to hit her. She grabbed the phone to call for help. He grabbed the receiver out of her hand and hit her around the head with it. The resulting black eye was embarrassing. The ladies at work knew her family circumstance, knew her dad, and although she wasn't aware of it, they were really concerned. When she went to work the next day they asked her about the black eye. This was the last time her dad hit her. Annie was seventeen.

How could she tell them her dad hit her with the telephone, without appearing to be a naughty girl, again?

Annie was convinced people thought she was a very naughty girl and deserved it.

She wasn't really a naughty girl. She didn't deserve the hiding, especially as she'd never peeped into any window at anyone. The idea didn't even enter her mind.

But in those days, adults were right, and kids had no rights. Tina was seventeen.

Her boyfriend came to the rescue that night.

As often happened when her dad was angry, no matter what the hour, he had a shower, changed clothes and was ready to go out. While he was distracted, Annie jumped into his car and drove to her boyfriend's house. When she explained what had happened, he followed her back to her dad's place, so she could return his car.

On their way back to her boyfriend's place, the Police pulled them over and told them her dad was charging her with illegal use of a motor vehicle. They told the Police Officer the car had already been returned to the carport. The officer persuaded Annie's dad to drop the charges. It would have been an interesting case, had it made it to court.

Annie spent the night at her boyfriend's house. At the recommendation of the Police Officer, she settled in to board with his family, and his father helped her buy her first car. Once again, the decisions were made for Annie.

It was the late sixties, the time of the Vietnam War and National Service.

Annie's boyfriend was called up to the army and headed interstate for basic training.

Annie's social life changed. She met new people and she started going out more. She had new freedom with her car, and became used to the concept of being popular. She revelled in the attention. Annie became so "popular", she became pregnant.

People were still making decisions for her. Annie moved back to her dad's house, but she was feeling alone and hopeless. A handfull of anti-depressants looked like a good option. Her dad came home earlier, and saw the left over pills on the floor. So he mixed some warm salt water for Annie to drink, so she'd vomit. He then took her to the local hospital for observation. The staff was very understanding and helpful.

Reflecting back to these times, Annie felt this whole period of her life was surreal.

CHAPTER 7

SEX EDUCATION

The first day of the Christmas School Holidays, at the end of her primary school years, aged eleven and a half, Annie noticed blood in her knickers. She furtively went to her Grandmother to report her findings, not knowing what to expect.

Without any explanation, her Grandmother went into panic mode and tail spins, and proceeded to sift through the scrap material basket in the linen cupboard.

Annie's Nanna did a lot of sewing and dressmaking, and the left over fabrics were rolled up and stored in the basket for likely future use.

She began cutting and sewing a belt and pads out of a roll of cream coloured flannelette cotton.

No shop-bought pads and belts for this little girl. Annie only found out about sanitary napkins after her grandmother died. The discovery of tampons came much later.

As the needle of the Singer treadle machine rhythmically pierced the fabric of the first pad, and without looking up from her work, Annie's grandmother uttered these fateful words, "Now stay away from boys!"

She also gave a vague explanation of the regularity of the occurrence, thereby identifying Annie's malady as a period. She'd begun her menstrual cycle. She wasn't sure how she should feel. Was it a good thing or a bad thing? Was it something she'd done to cause it?

Now Annie began the steepest learning curve of her life. Out of the little protective world her grandmother had built around her, into the great unknown, of the real world.

The reason for her Nanna's panic was later explained. "Your mother was fifteen when she started." Like Annie had some control over it, and once again did it wrong.

And then Nanna told Annie a little story about a silk handkerchief. The "protection" of her day.

Annie recalled the story as her grandmother told it, about the time she spent with a man in her younger years. No mention of the man being her grandfather.

The man apparently wooed her grandmother, and when they consummated their relationship the young man used a silk handkerchief as a condom.

In her later years, Annie's mind could only picture the association, relationship, connection of her grandmother and the man, but she wondered about lubrication of the flimsy fabric, the reliability of the flimsy fabric, and with a smirk on her face, she wondered about the position of the knot securing the flimsy handkerchief to the man's penis

Annie could only imagine. She shuddered.

Meanwhile, Annie felt like she was cursed in some way, but then rationalised it by thinking, *"Elizabeth Taylor and the movie stars must also get periods"*.

It meant nothing to Annie at the time, but it became much more significant as she entered adolescence, went to secondary school, and started socialising with boys.

She'd mixed mostly with the four other girls in her class at primary school, but she didn't have much to do with boys, other than the regular game of hide and seek which involved the entire school.

Annie remembered her dad warning her to be careful which boys she befriended at the time. There was no explanation, just the warning.

She later learned her biological father had two sons. They lived in the same community and were then at girl-chasing age. These details were covered up for more than forty years.

"No wonder everybody was nervous and protective!" Annie thought.

Annie wasn't really aware of herself, or her appearance. Her Grandmother was always well-dressed, matching the hat, gloves, shoes and hand bag, and she dressed Annie fashionably for each occasion.   There was no emphasis on vanity or personal appearance, but her outfit had to be fashionable.

She remembered the annual shopping expedition to the city. Her grandmother would pick out some items for Annie to try, but Annie never made the decision which outfit she wanted to wear.

Apart from attending school in a uniform, Sunday service and Sunday school were the social events Annie attended the most. Her Grandmother dressed her in the "correct" way, to ensure Annie's appearance reflected her grandmother's level of care, to the church community.

Annie knew nothing about lipstick and powder. She wasn't aware she had very crooked and decayed teeth.

She must have had some appeal and attraction to some of the boys. Being a shy but very friendly, naive girl probably did it.

Annie became very close to a boy from high school. He was a year or two older, but he seemed to be drawn to her, and Annie began to enjoy the attention and kisses they shared whenever the opportunity presented itself.

Another boy at High School was also attracted to Annie, but only at school. The friendship faded with time.

The relationship with her school friend deepened when she stayed in town with a great aunt while her grandmother was in Hospital for minor surgery. Annie and her friend would go bush walking to spend private time together. This time was spent talking, kissing and cuddling, which was enough for them at the time. Annie didn't know anything else; she only knew about "this stuff" from television and movies.

Annie was raised in a strong Christian community which German immigrants settled in the mid eighteen hundreds.

Much of the history of the Lutheran Church in Australia began in this district, and Annie's grandparents were staunch, faithful and recognized members.

Annie's "fear" of men and sex was strictly embedded by the teachers, at church and at home. So going beyond kissing and cuddling were definitely never considered. Annie was too afraid to do more. The fear of pregnancy was more like terror of the unknown. *"Can I get pregnant from kissing?"*

That was until she was left alone with her trusted, loving grandfather.

Annie trusted and loved her Papa and followed him to the shed, the blacksmith shop, the paddock to check the sheep, or go fishing in the farm dam. He taught Annie how to cast a hand line and to reel in the red fin perch which inhabited the large dam. She'd do anything to spend time with him to help with his hobbies and projects in the shed

At the age of twelve, the relationship changed somehow. Indirectly at first, but he became more invasive and insistent in a very short time.

He'd insist Annie "play" with him under the table after tea, as her grandmother sewed and they all watched I Love Lucy or some other program on the black and white television.

TV was very new and black and white, but Annie was only allowed to watch it after her homework and chores were completed to her grandmother's satisfaction.

Annie's grandfather's attentions seemed to be forced on her at every opportunity, even when her nanna was in the house - even in the same room.

Annie never knew if her grandmother knew what her grandfather was doing to her.

Her grandparents seemed to have a very active sex life, according to the rhythmic squeaks coming from the bedroom most mornings.

Her Papa even showed her how he used the toilet to pee. She never thought for a minute it was wrong. While he never penetrated her, he would tell her to stand on a step and then place his penis between her thighs. She tried to please him in the way he wanted to be pleased because she loved him and didn't dare refuse and disrespect her elders.

If Annie had told her grandmother or any of the family about her Papa's behaviour, she believed she would have been accused of lying. She may have even been punished for lying and not respecting her elders. She didn't dare take the risk. Annie remained silent.

She was in her thirties before she even admitted to herself what he did was wrong. Then she felt the guilt of allowing it to happen. Until then, Annie believed it wasn't really bad because it was her much respected grandfather, and she consoled herself with the fact he didn't ever have sex with her. This socially upstanding adult had taken advantage of her innocence, fragility and trust. She never forgot, although she did eventually forgive.

She spent her whole life trying to please those around her, the family, her father, her boyfriends, her husband, and later on, her abusive partner.

And so, with her need to be cuddled, kissed, and loved stir, Annie shared her feelings with many. She was ignorant of the consequences of her actions and did not know she was being promiscuous.

After Annie left college at the age of seventeen, she became sexually active with a long-term boyfriend. The pair was very close, but very naive. They continued their relationship without protection, and it was just luck she didn't get pregnant.

Annie's boyfriend was called up for national service. She really missed him and her need for attention intensified during his absence. She began socialising in a new circle of friends.

To relieve the loneliness and prolong the attention, she had sexual relationships with two of these new friends, and then she was pregnant.

Her fiancé, still in the Army, was shattered and bitter. Who could blame him? She'd betrayed him in the worst possible way.

Annie didn't realise the severity of the impact her pregnancy had on those around her. She couldn't understand why her life changed so dramatically.

Annie knew she'd done wrong, but didn't quite know how wrong. Her innocence was gone, but she didn't know how she lost it. Termination was not an option at the time.

Her father severely reprimanded her, and sent her off to the Church for forgiveness. Annie had no comprehension of what it all meant and no one ever explained it, not even the Minister.

Annie was very naive in her understanding of life. At eighteen she was expecting a baby.

When everything seemed to be beyond her, she took a handful of prescribed tranquilisers to solve her problems and to free herself from her dad's judgement.

Fortunately, her dad arrived home on time to find some tablets on the floor. He forced her to vomit before the tablets could affect her. She was admitted to hospital for two weeks until she felt stronger.

Depression was to be her constant companion – she felt lost and miserable. Annie had no real concept of what was happening to her, and no one seemed to be on her side with her psychological and physical.

Annie's dad took her to the baby's father's place, but Annie stayed in the car and was not aware of what transpired in the house. All she knew the baby's father didn't want to know about her and the baby. No one offered help and support, only judgement. Annie was very confused.

Her fiancé had demonstrated his hurt and justifiably ended the relationship. She was judged as a very bad girl by the extended family and relatives. One of her girlfriend's parents stopped her from being friends with Annie. Maybe they thought their daughter was going to catch what Annie had. They never knew their daughter introduced Annie to this new social scene.

Her dad offered to marry her, to save face. When Annie's silent shock and disgust subsided, she wondered how she could decline her dad's proposal without seeming disobedient and disrespectful. What could this naive, compliant teenager say to her dad? She cautiously discussed it and then declined. It was never mentioned again. The memory stayed with her until long after his death, forty years later. She still felt contempt and disgust at the memory.

She was in a very lonely place. She was alone in a hostel for unmarried mothers – a house full of strangers, with unwanted pregnancy in common.

Annie had to spend the next six months at the hostel, doing her duties as all the other residents did. Some worked in the laundry, some worked in the kitchen. She cleaned the hostel and later she was promoted to clean the maternity hospital section upstairs.

She spent many nights alone, awake and distressed. Depression inflicted itself upon her most of the time, as it had since the sudden death of her grandmother four years before.

It was all too late to remember her grandmother's words, "Now stay away from boys."

Annie gave birth to a beautiful, seven pound, twelve ounce girl. While she had resigned herself to adopting the baby out, she was determined to spend time with her little girl for the two short weeks they had together.

Her dad and the controlling, tyrannical aunty decided it would be in nineteen year old Annies's best interest for her to stay with the aunty. In those days "good girls" didn't live alone in a flat. So the decision of where nineteen year old Annie was to live was once again made for her.

CHAPTER 8

BACK ON TRACK

Annie applied for a job at the quarry up the road from her aunty's and uncle's farm. Her job was to operate the weighbridge and do the accounts. She loved the job and enjoyed the camaraderie with the workers and the truck drivers.

Some of them invited her to join them on their table tennis team. It involved one night of training and then match night, which took them to different towns around the district. Annie really enjoyed it and she was surprised by her own ability as her game improved.

Once again, no one at home took any interest in her hobbies or interests. The only interest they showed was in whoever picked her up and dropped her off. Her aunty's greatest interest was to know who was hooning and did wheelies in the yard, which disturbed the gravel on the driveway.

The driveway was on a slight hill in a roundabout style around a couple of cypress trees. It was almost impossible to not disturb the gravel on the upward track of the yard.

Annie passed the instructions on to whoever picked her up, and of course it was like a red rag to a bull. As they drove out of the yard, the young, cheeky drivers took great delight in stirring the gravel with their cars.

They'd rev the engine and accelerate to get the most out of the wheelie, and to spray gravel up against the garage wall. It made Annie smile, but she knew she would suffer the consequences of their actions.

Her aunty punished Annie for their antics. She was made to do jobs around the yard after she'd walked the mile home from work.

Once again Annie suffered for something she hadn't done, and had no control over.

Her aunty would even phone the lads' parents complaining about the gravel stirring incidents. Obviously the message was passed on, because the gravel was strewn even higher and wider on their next visit. Some of the boys were even banned from entering the driveway, and they had to drop Annie off at the end of the driveway. She had to negotiate a cattle grid, and walk down the steep, dark driveway to get to the house.

In the morning Annie would feel her aunty's wrath before walking to work at the weighbridge. In the cold, wet winter she'd wear rubber boots, a rain coat, a hat, and carry an umbrella. She'd be cold and wet when she arrived at work. At no time did anyone from the family offer to give her a lift to work or home. She'd have to sit out the day by the heater, in the cold office. When the drivers went to the open window to receive the docket for their load, the cold wind would rush right on in. Even the heater couldn't take the chill out of the winter's damp air.

Annie also walked home in the cold rain. On more than one occasion her aunty would drive into the yard a few minutes after she arrived home. The timing seemed just too close to be coincidental. Getting home to the smouldering wood fire was welcome relief from the icy cold

Annie thought she may have been too harsh in her judgement on the first couple of occasions, but when the "coincidence" recurred more often over time, she concluded it was probably deliberate. Perhaps her aunty was trying to teach her a lesson in the hardships of life, or she was ensuring Annie had her exercise. Why else?

Maybe it was to punish Annie for all her, and maybe even her mother's past deeds. Perhaps it was to teach her a lesson in respect for her elders? Or maybe it was to make her suffer to toughen her up. Maybe it was all of these things.

Her aunty was a staunch churchgoer, and ran the family with a firm, dominant, critical hand. She didn't see the good in too many people but could see their faults with judgemental accuracy. Woe betide anyone who disagreed with her, or entered into a defensive debate.

This aunty was very critical of everything or what she didn't understand. This raised another confusing issue for Annie who had been taught to "judge not".

Annie's aunty could be very harsh and held a grudge with a very firm grasp. What she didn't understand or agree with, she feared and condemned.

She treated Annie with the same disdain. There was no kindness or caring shown, just domination and control, in an effort to turn Annie into a good, obedient girl.

Initially Annie believed her aunty had taken her in as an act of kindness and obligation after she had the baby, and went through the adoption process, but Annie never saw the kindness.

Despite paying board, Annie was supposed to demonstrate her gratitude at every opportunity, even when she'd been upset by her aunty's actions and behaviour.

While doing the dishes one night, Annie found it very difficult to feel grateful. She was being threatened with a glass bottle waving over her head, as her aunty was trying to compel Annie to read prayer books.

While drying the dishes one evening, her aunty screamed, "You *have* to read your prayer books! You *have* to read your prayer books!"

Annie believed no one could write what she was feeling. She believed it was between her and God, but her well-meaning aunty couldn't accept the concept.

Annie tried to express her feelings about prayer books but was shut down. It was prayer books, or else!

Meanwhile, Annie's uncle sat silent at the table, reading the newspaper.

There was never a shortage of prayer books. Annie received them for every birthday and Christmas from the time she could read.

Annie had always dreaded this aunty because she thought she was a controlling, tyrannical woman – but her opinion was softened about forty years later.

CHAPTER 9

THE LAST WORD

Annie saw a frail, elderly, troubled woman, who knew all the history of her own family, and all her near and distant relatives. Who married whom, where they lived, how many children and what they were doing with their lives.

Her aunty, now over eighty years old, had eleven brothers and sisters. She was now living with her husband, Annie's uncle - Annie's mother's brother. He was patient, quietly spoken and still a stickler for detail, as Annie remembered him. He used to fly small planes and was passionate about flying. His only son continued the tradition.

They knew the saga of Annie's life, how she fitted into this family right from the beginning. They knew about the arranged marriage between Annie's mother and her dad, yet no one ever spoke a word about it. No one asked Annie about her feelings. It was all just covered up, shoved under the carpet, and life went on.

As Annie went through life, the saga monopolised many of her thought-filled hours. To spare anyone any embarrassment, or to avoid resurrecting any ghosts, she never raised the subject with her closest family.

During her most recent visit, uncle inspected Annie's vehicle with a critical eye and a fine tooth comb, while her aunty questioned her ability to manage her large four wheel drive, and how she'd acquired these skills.

This man was one of her closest relatives. They'd shared the same house and meal table for many years, but still he knew nothing about her adult life. He'd never made any effort to keep in contact over the years, to take any interest in her welfare, lifestyle, or her youngest two children. They had involved themselves in her eldest daughter's life after Annie left her first marriage.

Because Annie always felt guilty about her younger years, she didn't keep contact with them either. She actually avoided this family. Annie feared the judgement.

Annie felt disappointment, which represented itself as a blank in her life. She'd had a full and complicated life, and managed it all alone with no family support. She never asked for it. It was never offered.

Annie explained how she had helped her husband when he worked on cars. She told them she had helped her former partner recondition an engine by manually grinding valves, holding parts while he attached or detached them.

Annie told them she could even change tyres on her vehicles - the four wheel drive, and the large caravan she travelled with and lived in.

She told them she had to be very resourceful during her second relationship with her partner, a truck driver and commercial fisherman. He would be away from home for long periods, leaving her to do minor maintenance and repairs around the house and the car. Then, in later years as a single mother, she had to do what she could without spending much of the meagre Single Parent Benefit.

Annie also explained her experiences on cattle stations and bush driving, "and anyway, it's got power steering," she told them.

They seemed to accept her explanations without too much judgement.

Annie left feeling she had closed another chapter in her book of life. She had faced and survived the visit with her tyrannical, controlling aunty without a scratch, and no glass bottles were shattered in the duration of this visit.

CHAPTER 10

A DREADED VISIT

Annie mused as she buckled up the seat belt and started her car, *"It wasn't so bad. I survived".*

"In fact, I quite enjoyed it. Their quirkiness was amusing", she thought as she reversed out of the driveway.

Now more mature, experienced and open minded, able to make up her own mind and stand up for herself, Annie finally faced her nemesis - her dreaded, tyrannical aunty, her tormenter through her childhood and later teenage years. Aunty used to wait until Annie's grandmother was out in the garden or in town on business, and then inflict her version of discipline with a strap.

Annie's grandmother threw the leather strap into a creek on the road to the city. *"Nana, and nana alone administered the discipline",* she reasoned.

Her uncle, this aunty's husband, was still the wise old calculator who always thought things through. He spent ages during her visit, calculating her fuel consumption in miles per gallon, from kilometers per litre. He took great interest in her four wheel drive vehicle and the tools and equipment Annie carried with her.

He retired from farming, which had been his life since childhood. They grew potatoes, lucerne for hay, but the main source of income was dairy cows – one hundred and twenty of them.

Annie had been on the road towing her caravan, fulfilling a thirty year dream of travelling around Australia. Her travels so far had taken her down the west coast of Australia, across the Nullarbor Plain to eastern South Australia.

While in the area, Annie took the opportunity to visit relatives and family, to get some answers to her questions about her mother's life leading up to her death. Annie may have even found an explanation of some of her hereditary, chronic health issues. She knew they weren't from her mother's side of the family.

Annie's elderly aunty shuddered when she saw the big vehicle, and without taking a breath kept saying, "I couldn't drive a big thing like that! It's a bulldozer. How do you back it? Who parks it? Why such a big van? What about traffic? What about maintenance? Who taught you?"

"Certainly not you", Annie thought to herself with a smile.

If they'd taken any interest in Annie's life instead of judging and condemning her, they would have known what her capabilities were - they'd know her.

Annie grew up with these people in the same house and farm until the age of fourteen, yet they didn't know her.

Instead they'd been standing in judgement and crucifying her, without ever asking her about the circumstances - especially after Tina left her husband and eleven month old daughter.

They didn't attempt to contact her to ask why, if they could help, or if she needed support. Just judgement!

"If they'd taken an interest in her life and her welfare, they may have learned it was partially due to the way they treated her which made her such an insecure person", Annie reflected.

At the time she didn't even believe in herself enough to be a mother to her baby girl.

"I knew how to give babies away, but I didn't know how to keep them", Annie reflected.

Annie's husband was a thoughtful, gentle man, but he had been brought up to depend on his mother and to be dominated and demoralized by his father. What hope did their marriage have?

Annie didn't feel adequate as a wife or mother.

Annie thought there was nothing to be gained by resurrecting the past, much as she would have loved to. She really wanted to let loose and remind them, especially this aunty, of how they treated her and how she felt at the time.

Instead, she had driven up the driveway of their suburban house and rung the front door bell with a little apprehension.

Annie greeted her aunty with a smile on her face and her head held high as the door opened.

Seeing this elderly, frail couple doing things in the same pedantic way they had always done, or perhaps even more so, Annie just couldn't do it. She couldn't be angry, bitter or vindictive anymore. She'd grown up and put much of her past behind her.

This frail, judgemental woman had no idea of the damage she had done psychologically to Annie in the past. Annie now believed her aunty couldn't do anymore damage.

While Annie covered her feelings, there was nothing to be gained by chucking all her anger into their faces.

She had moved on in the knowledge she survived mentally and physically in spite of their bullying.

"I'm not a naughty, lazy girl, and probably never was," Annie told herself, *"She had me convinced for all those years"*.

Annie now only felt sorry for her aunty. Her life had been filled with the malicious judgement of others, while she appeared to live the life of a caring, Christian, on a very lucrative farm.

It's not for me to judge", Annie told herself. *"I have forgiven her and moved on"*.

CHAPTER 11

LEAVING LOVE BEHIND

So many things in Annie's life led to her marriage - and her separation.

In her teenage years she'd given a child away, as a result of a short relationship which concluded as an illegitimate pregnancy.

She then lived with a judgemental, controlling aunty and passive uncle.

It seemed she was always living in a place where they wanted to control her, to teach her a life lesson.

At nineteen, Annie was living under the same conditions as she did as a child, and this aunty persisted in treating her the same way.

All her life, Annie believed whatever she did was never good enough for the adults around her. She never cleaned her room right. She didn't do her chores around the house the way her aunty demanded she did them.

When Annie lived with her grandmother she was taught how to clean venetian blinds, louvre windows and skirting boards.

It seemed to be much more than a life lesson on how to keep a house. To Annie it seemed like absolute control – orders instead of requests. Punishment, instead of explanation and patience. There was only one way to do it – aunty's way.

Annie was lonely and felt urged to escape all of it.

She had her full time job. Her sport was her social life. She didn't have a car, and she didn't have any close friends to share time with or confide in.

Annie spent time with her cousin, who was six years younger than her. They'd kick the football around the yard if there was any daylight time between chores.

Her young cousin was given everything. Spoilt and coddled to a sickening degree. The indulgence extended to music lessons, whether he wanted them or not. They bought him a very expensive instrument to practice on, and of course, to play when anyone visited. The poor young bugger had no say in the matter. No one ever asked him either. In his adult life, despite his mother's disapproval, he went on to be very successful in his chosen career, and marriage, and never played music again. Annie pitied him, but never envied him.

She needed to escape all of it. "Nice" girls didn't live in flats or have their own car.

Annie needed someone of her own. She'd met a nice man a year or so before. He was a "nice country boy" with a good job, who really loved football and cricket and actively supported them in his home town.

So she wrote to him just to touch base. He wrote back, and their friendship developed into much more. He lived quite a distance away, so they'd spend the weekends together, either at his place or at her aunty's house – in separate rooms, of course. They'd go to footy, the drive-in movies, local dances, friends houses, church, or just go for drives together.

Annie decided this "nice man" would be a good husband. He was a quieter sort of person and was very popular within the community. His father dominated their household and was extremely mean with his money. He was so tight!

Annie always had visions of the old man lying in his coffin with his hands clasped tightly around two paper bags full of cash. She was sure he was going to take it with him. He didn't.

Her "nice man" was wise with his money, but never mean.

After going out for about a year, they became engaged and were married in a family celebration the following year. Annie cried from the time she walked down the aisle until the ceremony was over. She never understood whether it was joy, relief, or embarrassment at being the centre of good, happy attention.

They bought a house in his small home town. He worked at a local garage, and she found casual work at the local take-away.

Their lives were full, and happy. They worked on the house renovations and the garden together.

After over a year, Annie and her husband were excited to learn she was pregnant. In the early stages, when everything was going well, they packed up for a driving holiday half way around the country.

When their baby daughter was born, she became the centre of Annie's life, while her husband was very reluctant to be involved - even reluctant to hold their infant child.

It was the way it was in those days. It was the woman's job – house and baby.

The men just bragged to their mates and celebrated the pending parenthood, while the wife huffed and puffed for hours in the labour ward. Of course, pain was overtaken by ecstatic relief and everyone began the celebration immediately after the birth.

His mean, miserable father softened, and took to the child with more affection than anyone had ever seen him give. The old man would go over to their house with any excuse, to spend time with the baby. It really was a miracle to see how the old man had changed.

The grandmother would visit daily. This quiet spoken, humble woman would bring food over for the meals, or vegetables and eggs from her chooks and garden.

Somehow Annie began to feel inadequate. His mother meant well, but Annie believed her mother-in-law was being critical and demeaning, implying Annie wasn't good enough or capable of providing for her family.

Annie did have moments of what she believed was laziness and at times felt overwhelmed by house, garden and family. She became depressed as she had done four years before, and began to feel the loneliness again.

She didn't understand her own emotions, so how could anyone else, especially her husband understand and offer her support.

Once again she needed more cuddles than her husband was even aware she needed. She rarely initiated any demonstrations of affection. Annie felt neglected and unwanted.

The guilt and inadequacy became overwhelming. She went away for a holiday to see a long-time friend. Annie left her much loved eleven month old child behind with her husband and his mother. She was only going to be away for a week. *"Besides,"* she thought, *"They'll look after the baby better than I can"*.

After the break Annie just couldn't go back. She told her husband she'd take another week, and he didn't ask when she was coming home. Annie only returned to pick up some personal belongings and to spend some time with her much-loved child.

It was another year before Annie saw her little girl again. She'd left another child behind – the second.

It wasn't because she didn't love her child, it was because she felt she wasn't a good enough mother and wife. She felt she just didn't belong.

The need to run, and keep moving continued to be Annie's torment for most of her life, but the need to be cuddled and loved diminished when the memories of her earlier promiscuous years haunted her.

Once again, everyone who knew Annie stood in judgement, condemning her decisions and lifestyle. No one ever asked her why, or offered support or assistance. She was once again on her own, by choice. The decision was based on her belief she wasn't good enough as a person. It was more peaceful to be alone than to be judged and condemned.

Running away was the only way Annie knew how to conceal her true feelings and what she really wanted. She couldn't face those who she thought didn't support or love her. She didn't know she needed help, and even if she did, she didn't know how to ask for it.

In time, she became strong enough to talk to her ex-husband and explain what caused her to leave. He was more understanding than she'd ever given him credit for. They remained good friends, sharing family celebrations, even after he remarried.

Annie's eldest daughter lived with her grandmother, her father's mother, until she became a rebellious teenager. When her behaviour threatened to get out of hand it was agreed she should live with her mother and her two younger half sisters from Annie's second long-term relationship.

The reunited family was tentative with each other at first and Annie's teenager, almost a stranger, took a little while to settle into her new home, new school in a new town, with her new family - her mother and her sisters.

After a heated discussion at three o'clock one Sunday morning, the hung-over teenager began to accept her new lifestyle. From then on she made new friends and supported her two younger sisters.

Having her exhusband's and their daughter's forgiveness was the strong start Annie needed to get on with her life. She could now forgive herself.

Annie's teenager grew up to be a beautiful young woman and the strong, hard working mother of two boys.

Her relationship with the boy's father also broke down because of his abusive behaviour toward her.

Annie's daughter endured months of demoralising abuse. It escalated from verbal to physical, before she mustered up the strength and confidence to take their two boys and escape the violent, confidence-crushing situation.

CHAPTER 12

ALL FOR LOVE

Annie didn't get much love and cuddles as a child and adolescent. Everyone was too busy trying to raise her to be an obedient child by telling her how bad she was, how naughty she was, and how lazy she was, without explanation, understanding or support. They probably hoped she would suddenly see the error of her ways and stop being "naughty" and "lazy".

She spent the rest of her life trying to prove them all wrong. Annie kept her distance from relatives for many years and tolerated abuse from her second long-term life partner, without telling anyone.

Annie felt obliged to stay in the long-term abusive relationship because she felt guilty about leaving her first husband, their child, and stuffing up the marriage.

If he accused her of doing something wrong she now believed and accepted she deserved to be punished. Annie was resigned to the abuse. She was determined to stick with him, until she got it right.

She really loved this man. When sober, he was loving, caring, and a lot of fun. They worked and loved together in various places around the country before they settled down and had children. They sang together at family and friend gatherings.

Even on their first date, he accused her of not looking at him enough while she was dancing with one of his mates. He slapped her around when they were home, and Annie had no idea what she'd done to offend and upset him. Nothing she said to defend herself would stop him yelling accusations and hitting her.

He also accused her of having an affair while he was working away for weeks at a time. If he had been home more often when he wasn't away working, instead of at the pub, he would have known what she was doing with her time. She put up with it for almost nine years. Annie later realized it was all about his jealousy and insecurity. After being punished as a child, Annie thought she must have done something to upset her partner, and she deserved to be punihed.

When he was supposed to be home, he spent most of his days drinking in the pub. He wouldn't even come home for meals. He would only come home when the pub closed at midnight.

He sometimes dragged Annie out of bed to accuse her of something he'd heard in the pub, or to throw her around the house. He would not accept her response and defence.

About three o'clock one morning he threw his pregnant partner out of bed ordering her to, "Get the watermelons out of the car!"

"What watermelons?" the sleepy Annie asked.

"Just get those fuckin' watermelons out of the car!" he roared.

Annie had no idea what he was talking about, but she obediently went out to the car, lifted the three very large, heavy watermelons out of the car's boot, and carried them into the house.

Apparently they'd "fallen off the back of a truck" parked in the pub car park into the car boot, while he was in the pub.

This man had the happy knack of scoring all kinds of goods and chattels through other pub friends. He even found work for himself and Annie when they were looking.

When the watermelons were settled into the kitchen, on top of the deep freezer, he kept yelling and raving, and then grabbed a carving knife out of the drawer.

Annie was terrified as he took his drunken, blind rage out on the melons. He slashed the three watermelons into small chunks, and began throwing them at Annie.

Slashed watermelon has very sharp edges, and hurling it across the room by a very strong man causes lacerations, welts and bruises. Watermelon slush flooded the kitchen floor and splattered the walls.

He settled down to eat the cold meal she'd prepared the previous evening. Then he went to bed, oblivious to the mess he'd made or the injuries he'd inflicted on his pregnant partner.

It took Annie two hours to clean up the majority of the mess on the floor so the other people in the household wouldn't slip and fall. She left the splatter on the walls.

When he finally dragged himself out of bed much later in the morning, he asked Tina, "What's that stuff up the walls?"

Annie took great delight in telling him. He didn't seem to notice the lacerations, welts and bruises which were very obvious all over her body. He never did ask her about them.

When the bashings became more violent and more frequent, the Police considered it a private matter and wouldn't help. By the time domestic violence was an offence, Annie was too scared to leave because she had two children to consider. He used to threaten to hurt her, and told her to leave, but he said she couldn't take the girls.

Annie was panic-stricken with the idea of leaving her beautiful babies behind. In those days, womens' shelters were not an ideal option for temporary refuge.

She eventually gathered up the nerve to plan the secret escape with the children.

Annie convinced her partner she wanted to return to work. So she organised for a family friend to care for the children while she was at work. She bought a small station wagon and found work as a courier, which gave her a vehicle to escape in, and ultimately, some independence.

Initially, she stayed with a work mate until she was on her feet and found somewhere for her family to live.

The two bedroom unit Annie rented was comfortable and safe.

They hid for a few weeks, but Annie was determined the girls would know their dad. What he had done to her was between them, and nothing to do with the children. Annie never spoke about their father's drunken, abusive behaviour when they were within earshot.

Annie shared the first Christmas with their dad and his girlfriend, at a family gathering, so they could be together for the girls. It was a happy time. The fear she had felt didn't seem so intimidating. She still felt apprehensive, but the fear was gone. He had a new girlfriend to bash - and he did.

During the festivities, he asked her if their eldest daughter could stay with him and his new girlfriend for the holidays. They lived about eight hundred kilometers away.

Annie believed it would only be for the school holidays, but he had other plans. She learned her ex had planned to keep their daughter with him indefinitely.

At first she was resigned to the idea. In fact, she covered up her disappointment by convincing herself that it would be easier to care for just one child on her own. Deep inside, her heart was broken and she was afraid she may never see her child again. Annie didn't want to give another child away - the third.

Her second daughter, their eldest, lived with her dad and his partner and her son, for about four years, but the child saw how he abused his new girlfriend, and was even a victim herself. All brought on by grog, jealousy and insecurity. In Annie's mind nothing could justify the abuse.

By this time Annie and her youngest daughter were living in the same town as the child's father.

Annie didn't know the relationship between her ex and his girlfriend had ended, and her girl had been sent to his relatives in the city. He hadn't even talked to her about any new arrangements, or given her the opportunity to have her daughter living with her again.

When Annie learned from relatives he had planned to send their child to New Zealand, she panicked and worked very quickly to gain legal custody of the child as soon as possible.

As the relationship had been defacto, custody had to be decided by the Supreme Court at the time. After waiting nervously for three days, Annie was granted sole, uncontested custody of both of their daughters.

In the mean time a plan had to be set up for Annie to collect her daughter from the relative's house without anyone learning of her intention. It was almost abduction. The eight year old had no idea what she was about to endure.

With Police standing by and with the aid of her local church minister and Children's Services, Annie went to the relative's house to collect her daughter and her belongings.

The child was shocked and extremely confused by her mother's sudden appearance and all the unexpected activity. The relatives were also in shock, and didn't understand the urgency of the matter.

At first they refused to release the child, but when the Childrens' Services Officer explained, they packed her things and released her to Annie.

Although it was a victory for Annie, it was a traumatic victory for both of them. Her daughter took many months to recover from the distress her mother's actions caused. The tears eventually stopped and they talked about everything which she had experienced, whenever the child asked questions.

The family became very close as time passed and the little girl understood why her mother had to take such drastic actions at the time. She'd remembered seeing her father at his worst with his girlfriend.

Annie's daughter continued to maintain contact with her father, and a few years later she accompanied him to New Zealand to spend time with his relatives.

Annie always believed she did the right thing and made the best decision in a sensitive situation.

She raised the children on her own and worked hard at whatever job she took to support her family. She eventually ran her own business for about twelve years – from home at first. When both girls were in secondary school she moved into an office in town, rent free.

CHAPTER 13

NOT A WHOLE LOT OF LOVE

After all her disappointments and let downs, Annie believed she couldn't give all her feelings, trust and love to anyone - and only in moderation to her children.

No matter how much she wanted to love and let her feelings go, she thought she couldn't trust anyone with her innermost thoughts and emotions. Nor did she know how to accept love.

Annie believed her vulnerability and weakness would be used against her, and everything she'd worked for emotionally would crash around her. It was easier to stay detached, defensive and distant, than to be hurt or to be punished again.

She kept the barriers up. It would have taken a very understanding, loving compassionate person to earn her trust enough to remove the defenses.

Annie needed someone to trust her without question or judgement, to see her true, good qualities and support her through whatever life brought.

Alone, Annie would settle for a while but then the ghosts would rear their heads and her fears would come to the surface. It may not have been anything significant, just an off-the-cuff comment, but then the ghosts of insecurity would jump out and bite her on the bum.

If she went on a date with anyone, and he drank what she thought was too much grog, more than four drinks, the trigger would be fired. The terror of the memories of her dad and former partner, when they were drunk, would return causing her to dread what could happen.

Annie's dad was determined to always think the worst of her, as he'd apparently done with her mother since her death, or maybe before.

As a child Annie was never given the benefit of the doubt. There was no unconditional love, or any other kind.

Everything she did was questioned. She was punished for petty things like playing when she should have been getting the wood in or doing her homework. She had no right of defense or denial. The punishment often meant bearing the lashings of stick or strap. Little wonder she was quiet and shy, and didn't make any effort to defend herself.

These experiences were all very traumatic at the time, and again later in her life when she was forced to relive it with a violent partner. Annie was once again being belted for things she didn't do, and still no one believed her when she denied the accusations.

Many years later Annie sought medical advice for her mental distress and depression. She was then diagnosed with post traumatic stress disorder. At last! Some understanding and support.

It wasn't from family, but at least it was out there. There were times when Annie believed she was insane, or close to it.

As in any relationship, Annie believed she could trust her best friend and lover with her most private thoughts, without being judged or persecuted. Support, reassurance and cuddles were what she really needed, particularly from a male partner who could give her unconditional love, and whom she could trust and love unconditionally in return.

After more than twenty years, Annie was still alone, travelling alone, living alone. She knew she had the love of her children, but was it unconditional love?

CHAPTER 14

TOUGH LOVE

"Tough Love" intensely understated the feelings the mother felt, as she watched four strong policemen hold her "little" girl down on the ground, to bind her hands and feet with zip ties, while she thrashed around and screamed abuse at all within ear shot.

A large hole had been punched through a wall in the house. Annie had been screamed at and threatened. She had just been abused and held hostage by her own child - her fifteen year old daughter, and her boyfriend, for money.

Annie was absolutely distraught, and collapsed to the floor! A senior Police Officer stayed to comfort her. It took a long time and many cups of tea, to console her. The experienced senior Officer counselled Annie and tried to convince her it was not her fault. She took cold comfort in his words and continued to blame herself for many years after this experience.

Tina's youngest daughter continued to condemn her mother for many years, for not putting up with the violent, abusive, drug-induced behaviour. "You're my mother. You're supposed to put up with it."

The teenager was taken to the Police Station holding cells while arrangements were made to transport her five hundred kilometres by road, to the nearest juvenile detention centre in the city. Transportation by air was out of the question, because of the violent behaviour and disposition of the young teenager.

"When did she get so out of hand?" Annie asked herself.

"She was intelligent, very wise, but so rebellious," Annie reasoned.

According to the younger teenager, her behaviour and attitude was never her fault. She always made the wrong choice when it came to staying out of trouble, or getting involved. Then, when she was caught, it was always someone else's fault, usually Annie's.

Annie pondered the child's behaviour throughout her childhood and was at a loss to know how to come to terms with her personality. Annie never confided in anyone about how she felt, and would never admit to anyone she was having a hard time or not coping with her children. Annie believed she was a failure, reinforcing her childhood "conditioning".

She was too proud to admit she might even be a little bit defeated. Annie's pride and fear of criticism from anyone who knew her, prevented her from seeking support. She was terrified of being judged an unfit mother.

Annie recalled her youngest as a toddler. Up to the time she started school, she'd get into such bad moods it was difficult to reason with her. She would sometimes go into an uncontrollable rage.

This beautiful, bright, intelligent child had insisted on doing things "by herself" from the time she was a toddler. When Annie was unwell, her "baby" would tend to her mother's needs by supplying a glass of water and a tissue. Such tenderness and understanding from a two year old child directly contradicted the aggressive teenager she'd become.

Annie often wondered, *"Where did my child go? What generated the rage?"*

Annie used to hold her toddler tight and hug her until the mood passed and she went to sleep. After such an outburst, the child would be placid for a few weeks.

Early nights and getting enough sleep were definitely the cure.

As she got older and bigger, reasoning with her and controlling these outbursts and rages became more difficult for Annie.

Once her youngest child started going to school, others also had to cope and manage her behaviour. This created even bigger problems. It also created more problems within the family.

The first primary school sent the child into the "time out" room – for an entire term, every day. Her school work was always up to date.

Annie had numerous meetings with teachers and the school principal about the child's behaviour.

She constantly asked the school to keep the girl busy and to give her responsibility. She even went so far as to recommend they send her to the junior classes to help the little ones, or to read to the class, but nothing was ever done and the problem continued, even escalated.

Still Annie continued to persevere alone. No one wanted to listen or help, to understand, to reach and teach the child. It became a battle of wits between the teachers, the child and Annie.

She took her girls to counselling to help them all deal with this behaviour and to try to understand why. Once again, nothing was ever resolved and there was no treatment or "cure". The family even went to the Children's Hospital in the city to have the child assessed for any medical or psychological conditions but none were diagnosed.

The youngest used her intelligence to scam anything she could get for nothing, including trouble. She also used her "smarts" to fool her mother about her activities when she was out with her friends.

Annie trusted her girls were doing the right thing and in a safe environment at their friend's house. She was oblivious to the fact the friend's mother smoked copious quantities of dope and drank a fair amount of beer beyond "happy hour".

Annie had been to the house and met the parents, but she was really cranky with herself for missing the signs and not trusting everyone. After all, they were all parents of vulnerable, impressionable teenagers.

It took a long time for Annie to realise the girls had sold their Nintendo game for drugs.

The girls told Annie they were taking the game over to the house so their friends could play it over there. Annie shook her head in disappointment as she recalled her gullibility.

She berated herself thinking, *"Bloody hell! How dumb was I?"*

With only eighteen months between the girls, the gap in age closed with each birthday and they constantly competed with each other. The middle daughter was quieter and very tolerant of her youngest sister.

The youngest daughter criticised everything her big sister did. Her fashion sense, her friends, and later, her boyfriends. She became violent and often resorted to attacking her older sister.

While the two girls were close, they had very different personalities and attitudes. Most of the bickering was the result of jealousy and their differences. The older sister was in first year high school. The youngest was in year seven.

The youngest wanted to do everything her older sister was doing and didn't understand that different ages did different activities.

This behaviour caused Annie constant worry and she spent a lot of time struggling to keep the peace between the girls.

Annie suffered stress and migraine headaches and eventually chronic hypertension, which followed her for many years. Still the girls fought each other, without any thought for their mother.

Annie had tried very hard to stay out of their fights. She'd calmly hop in the car and go for a drive if she couldn't calm them down or tolerate it anymore.

As she walked out the door she would tell them, "I can't stand your fighting so I'm going out. The survivor can call the ambulance."

Annie would park somewhere nice and peaceful, turn the stereo volume up, close her eyes and let the music distract her.

Annie sought counselling for herself, to deal with her own reactions. She learned to love the child, but not accept the behaviour. It was the principle of "tough love".

Annie moved her family to a larger house on the other side of town, which meant the "problem" was that the child had to change schools.

Very early in the year Annie was called to meet with the principal of the new primary school. He explained her behaviour and how it affected the class and the teacher. She explained the hardships she had at home with the two girls.

The school principal and Annie agreed that he should deal with the child at school and that she should deal with the child at home.

The girl's attitude changed for the better for the first two terms. She still had her moments but at least she didn't go home frustrated and traumatised after being locked in a room all day, with nothing to do.

Most of the younger child's problems escalated when she was bored and frustrated, because no one bothered to ask her about her behaviour. She had to be busy. She thrived on responsibility.

Horses became a passion and she was a quick learner. The child became a proficient rider and faithfully cared for her animals. She was also a keen Netballer, but she stopped playing when she became good at it. Her reason was, "I'm sick of it."

Annie knew it was no longer a challenge at the level her girl was playing, and if she was to be promoted to a higher team she may not be as good. So she quit in case she failed.

A relief teacher stepped in when the principal went on long service leave. The acting principal had no idea how to deal with this Year Seven student. He was not prepared to negotiate with Annie, or the child. The problems and behaviours resurfaced with a vengeance.

In the third term, the acting Principal gave up and expelled her from the school. This was the ultimate indignation for mother and daughter. Annie was desperate. If the school couldn't support her, where would she go for support, advice, and assistance?

Fortunately Annie's eldest daughter was living in a nearby town, so the child went to stay with her during the week, to attend a small school in the district. It was the best time for the whole family.

As teenagers, the two girls fought over everything, and sharing the house with them became almost intolerable. Annie had no idea drugs were now involved.

Annie had to take break from all this stress, so the girls agreed to spend two weeks at a youth hostel. They continued to attend school and Annie saw them every day.

When they returned home, life was quite peaceful for a while, but as they grew into young ladies, their friendships spread beyond the group Annie was familiar with.

The troubled child was older, bigger and stronger, with a very determined attitude. Negotiation was almost impossible. She was too big to hold tight and hug until she went to sleep. When they were busier during the day, they became more tired by the end of the day, which was often the time for these outbursts. They had a bedtime curfew, but it seemed they did more in the night than sleep.

Annie's youngest daughter's behaviour became impossible by the age of thirteen and at secondary school.

The child couldn't cope with the new routine at secondary school - changing classrooms for lessons, being the "junior" at the new school. Different teachers, and a huge variety of personalities were very unsettling for her.

Annie's "baby" was transferred to a class of students who were experiencing difficulties with the routine and the environment. This strategy worked for a while. At least she wasn't wagging, and spending her days at the beach.

Annie happened to see her daughter walking down the street making a bee line for the beach and jetty where the locals used to swim.

"What's wrong with that?" you ask. In a teenager's ideal world, maybe, but there was no future in it.

The child didn't discuss her problems with her mother and the high school didn't report the problems until Annie asked how her youngest child was coping.

The two sisters were mixing with a group of friends from school. They spent a lot of time at their own house, so Annie knew where they were and what they did.

A local female Police Officer who knew Annie's family circumstances, approached her at a sporting event and in a genuinely, friendly gesture, asked Annie if the girls arrived home safely a couple of nights previous.

Annie didn't even know they'd been out. When Annie confronted her "little angels" about their midnight adventures two kilometres from home, they admitted to sneaking out with their friend who was sleeping over. Fortunately, it was just a teenage escapade which had a happy ending, but Annie shuddered at the thought of the frightening, alternative, possible consequences.

By now Annie was running her own business from an office in town. She had worked from home until the youngest child started high school and when her business expanded, she needed more space in a more prominent, accessible office.

The time had come for Annie to trust the girls to do the right thing. She had to trust she had raised the girls with enough responsibility and respect. However, she'd misjudged their level of responsibility and social activities.

It all went downhill during the second time in the youth hostel, almost twelve months later.

She treated them equally – if one went to the refuge house, they both went to the refuge. The older daughter understood Annie's logic but didn't like it much.

The unfortunate side was the older sister was caught up in all of the younger sister's activities. She wasn't the problem on her own, but together they just became too much for Annie to understand and manage. These issues often resulted in a fight – usually verbal, but sometimes physical.

Annie blamed herself, for being too strict and demanding, for putting too much pressure on herself and the girls to do it right. She was adamant she would not be a "typical" single mother, and her girls would be "good girls". Her girls were not going to be the product of a broken home and a dysfunctional family.

However, once again her youngest daughter got up to some mischief with the group and the girls "escaped" together.

In the mean time school was forgotten.

The girls moved to a "house of softer options", where two of their friends lived. The mother and her boyfriend smoked more dope than the other friend's parents, and didn't seem to take much interest in her own teenage boys' activities and behaviour.

Annie didn't approve of the girls' new residence, but there was little she could do.

By law the girls were now of the age when it was legal for them to leave home, with no consideration for the parent's standing in the matter.

A short time later, the Police informed Annie her youngest had been caught breaking into a building. The adventurous "team" caused senseless damage by smashing a window to get in, and throwing tea, coffee and sugar around the premises lunch room. The young girl was charged with "break and enter" and for stealing a "Bandaid" to cover the cut she sustained smashing the window. Annie laughed to herself at the irony, and thought, *"Karma. There is a God."* Annie showed no sympathy, but she was secretly torn inside.

The teenager continued to run amok and ended up in juvenile detention in the city. She just wouldn't learn it was her own behaviour which caused all her troubles.

The teenager was released from juvenile detention on a bond and was given community service. She opted to attend TAFE to upgrade her numeracy and literacy skills, which had been neglected during all the previous turmoil.

Like everything else, it worked for a while, and the teenager settled down with her boyfriend of the time.

The older sister came home to her mother on her own.

After this latest violent episode, the senior Police Officer reassured Annie, and convinced her she had no option but to have her daughter arrested and charged, to serve a second term in

70

juvenile detention. The teenager had to take responsibility for the consequences of her actions.

She had breached her bond and community service order from the previous break-in, band-aid stealing offence, and was charged with additional violent offences.

"Love the child – hate the behaviour!" Annie reminded herself as the helpful police officer left the house.

Her youngest was in juvenile detention and Annie had no idea when she was to be released, or where she would go. The police had advised Annie not to contact her because of the friction between them, and to show the youngster her mother really did not approve of her behaviour. The teenager blamed her mother for everything - especially for not tolerating her violent behaviour.

"You're my mother! You're supposed to love me anyway!"

The older daughter was settled in and "playing house" with her boyfriend, which was a relief for Annie at the time.

Annie's business was very demanding on her time. She felt she needed to take a break right away from home, and work.

After giving some thought to an advertisement in the daily newspaper, Annie applied for three months work on a Kimberley cattle station, as a housekeeper, cook and gardener.

"Hey, I can do that! How hard can it be? I've been doing it for years without pay", Annie thought, justifying her excitement.

She discussed the proposition with her family, before accepting the position. If all went according to plan, she would be back in time for the release of her youngest daughter from detention.

Annie went to work on the isolated, Western Australian cattle station.

CHAPTER 15

DRUG BUST

Somewhere along the way Annie's youngest daughter was introduced to hard drugs. It was just "grass" at first, then Crystal Methamphetamine, "ICE". This drug produced unpleasant psychotic behaviour in this strong-willed girl.

Her two older daughters smoked weed and probably tried other party drugs, but not enough to affect their lives. They all loved to go out dancing and enjoy a social drink.

In fact, Annie often thought, *"The less I know, the better. They're old enough to be responsible for their own lives and actions."* It was easier to remain ignorant in these matters.

She had done her best to educate them about drinking alcohol, smoking and drugs. Not to appear negligent, she'd taught them healthy living by example. They made their own choices. Annie did worry, but she kept it to herself. They always knew better. The ensuing argument was just as traumatic as the worry.

Before she settled down, Annie had worked in bars in fishing communities and saw some of the effects alcohol and drugs had on people. She didn't want to see her girls go down that path. They were adults now, and there was little she could do. She felt it was healthier for her to remain ignorant and not let it affect her life.

No matter what she believed, they wouldn't stop just because she said so. Annie relaxed in the knowledge the two older girls weren't into heavy alcohol or drug use. She consoled herself thinking, *"Two out of three's not bad."*

What was Annie to do? She was enjoying her independence, and knew she couldn't control her children now they had grown up and made their own lives.

Annie had spent the previous seventeen years putting her children first, making them her priority. She'd put her own life on hold, working hard, making a home for them and rarely going out socially.

She was determined to live by example - to be the role model for her children to aspire to. After all those years as a single, unsupported mother, Annie felt her job at home was done. She had worked hard, from home at first, and then from an office in town.

The girls were setting up house with their boyfriends. Not the sort of boyfriends Annie would have chosen, but they seemed to love and respect her girls, so what else could she do? She now had her own life to live.

The job in the Kimberley region of Western Australia suited her perfectly.

She had seen the region's spectacular coast about thirty years before from the deck of a prawn trawler, and had always wanted to return.

After discussing it with her three girls and gaining their approval, Annie headed out on her own, for the first time in seventeen years. On the long flight north, she felt her wings spreading with the jet's wings, holding her in the sky on the journey to her new life.

When the wet season shut down the station's cattle management activities, Annie found similar work and moved to another station, five hundred kilometres south.

She told the girls she wouldn't be returning home at the end of the initial four months. Annie really enjoyed the freedom and independence of the outback station life.

The youngest daughter came to visit the new station with the boyfriend of the time. He was a polite, well-mannered young lad, and Annie thought he was an ideal partner for her beautiful, intelligent, troubled child. The two visitors had a good time helping Annie with her duties around the homestead and riding station horses.

A few months later after Annie had moved into town, she learned the family's turmoil continued without her. Her youngest was pregnant, to a teenage boy who also had drug problems.

Annie was recovering from a work accident, so she had time to go back to attend the birth and help her "baby" care for her newborn baby.

Annie headed south near the time the baby was due. It was only a day or two later when Annie's first grandchild came into the world – a beautiful, healthy girl.

What a celebration! It was the happiest everyone had been for a long time. Annie's family reunited to support their sister and to welcome their new niece. They shared the joy and happiness together.

Even Annie's ex partner, the baby's grandfather, was present at the birth and joined in the celebrations. It really was one of Annie's happiest times.

Annie reflected, *"It's a shame these moments don't last and all the traumatic times forgotten."*

The new little family moved into a nice little house. Annie helped her daughter and new granddaughter settle into a routine.

At first she was a doting, loving mother. Annie hoped she would settle down, and get her "head on straight", but it wasn't to be. The euphoria crashed after Annie left to return north.

The baby's father had been out of the picture for some time leading up to the birth, but of course Annie was the last to know how and why. He also celebrated the birth of his daughter. The couple never reconciled, but he did take an active part in sharing time with his daughter, until her mother found better drugs, and another man to supply them. The baby's father ultimately gained custody.

Annie's family also became very adept at covering up the real story behind the story. It was the same when they lived at home as teenagers. She would probably never know the real truth about the relationships, the drugs and the lifestyle they led.

The young child stayed with her father for most of her first eight years.

Annie's middle daughter also spent a lot of time with the child and had a room for her niece at her house. They were very close, and their time together provided the only stability the child was to enjoy.

A foolish decision a few months later jeopardized any relationship they enjoyed.

The drugs brought on early labor - eleven weeks early, and the delivery of Annie's second grand daughter was by emergency caesarean. Royal Flying Doctor Service flew The baby to the city's Women's and Children's Hospital. She was placed in intensive care to gain strength and overcome drug withdrawal. The infant was strong like her mother, despite her immature lungs.

Until the birth, Annie had no idea her own baby was pregnant again. She had never met the drug-addicted boyfriend. By the time the baby arrived the pair had separated.

Her middle daughter filled her in on the recent events. Annie was shocked and distraught knowing there was nothing she could do. Her youngest had totally excluded her mother from any contact.

A few days after the birth, Annie's youngest daughter phoned her. She made menacing threats in a soulless, monotone voice, and then hung up. Annie couldn't remember the exact conversation. The only memory of the phone call was her daughter's tone and unpleasant accusations of neglecting her needs. Annie didn't even attempt to defend herself, or offer support or advice. Any trace of a relationship they may have had, was cut off with the click of the phone call ending.

It was another heart-breaking moment for Annie. She had another grandchild she would probably never see. Her youngest daughter had now chosen to be a complete stranger.

Annie was disappointed with her youngest daughter's decision to adopt, but reasoned it was probably the best for the child in the long run. Initially the baby was placed in long term, permanent foster care.

Annie hadn't heard any news of her youngest daughter for more than five years. In fact, it was her middle daughter who passed on the news.

The middle daughter had been entrusted with the information on the condition she didn't tell Annie where the little sister was, or give her any contact details.

Annie was relieved to learn her youngest had been clean and free from addiction for about three years, had steady, full time, long term employment, settled down with a new partner, and had resumed playing sport.

She was excited when told her youngest daughter had been reunited with the first child, now eight years old, as the father had relinquished custody.

In the mean time, Annie learned her youngest daughter had made arrangements to adopt the younger daughter to the foster parents. Annie believed the child represented an extremely difficult time in her life, and decided the foster parents should adopt the little girl.

The foster parents were wonderful and had a happy family of teenage boys. Now they had the confirmed permanent custody of "their little girl". They had always made the child's family welcome and encouraged them to be part of the little girl's life. They were a very special, loving family, and Annie was very grateful they were the adopting parents.

The "tradition" of giving her children away was being continued, but she believed the biological ties would never be broken. Her own experience with adoption was always present in her mind. She had made some effort to contact the child she gave birth to and adopted out more than thirty years before, without response.

Annie was thankful her daughter had survived her bad years and had settled down in a healthier, productive, happy life.

She also had peace of mind knowing her youngest maintained contact with her older sister and their own father.

She was resigned to the fact she may have to wait to see or talk to her grown up baby but, at the time, she was thankful her daughter was alive. Annie didn't want to undermine the relationship of trust between the sisters.

Annie loved her children dearly. She had forgiven herself for all the things she had done wrong in her own teen years and during their childhood. There is no rule book for parenting, single or otherwise.

She always kept an open heart and mind, and an open door for her children, no matter what they'd done. Her youngest chose to keep her distance, which hurt Annie, but she understood.

Annie was proud of the lifestyle she had cultivated to keep their lives as stable as possible. She had worked hard to give them a comfortable, organised life, and to live by example. She worked from home to be with the two younger girls, although it never seemed to be enough, especially for her youngest child. It was all a balancing act.

Annie concealed her disappointment and dealt with it by keeping some distance from her family. She felt, despite her efforts, she had let them down in many ways, and she should have, somehow, done better. She never discussed these feelings with her children until her middle daughter accused Annie of dressing them in "daggy" clothes and feeding them instant noodles.

Annie simply responded by saying, "At least your clothes were new, if not trendy, and you always had a snack after school before going to the stables, music lessons or sport training. There was always good food in the house but you were not always there to eat at meal times."

It hurt Annie to hear it was how her daughter felt.

Annie sent birthday and Christmas presents and tried to spend every second Christmas with her family. They had moved on and made their own ways in the world, and Annie didn't know where she fitted in.

She always felt guilty for her misdeeds as a teenager, and although she had spoken to her children about some of them, especially about adopting a baby out, she always believed she had set the pattern.

CHAPTER 16

COVERED LOVE

After many years on her own without a partner, Annie used to daydream about having someone with whom to share her life.

Annie didn't like it when people tried to impress her with "I am". She called it "a severe case of FIGJAM" – *"Fuck I'm Good, Just Ask Me!"*

She didn't like to wear the mask of makeup and cosmetics, and she wasn't a fashion victim just to keep up appearances. "No polly-filla or war paint for me," she'd say.

Annie was always a practical and realistic dresser, which was essential when living and working in a tropical climate, or in a cold climate with higher profile profession. When she did make the effort, she could be quite impressive. The trouble was she didn't make the effort very often. She dressed for the occasion and comfort.

Annie's past and all those adventurous jobs made her a very down to earth, open-minded understanding, honest person.

She believed talking was always the best way to learn and deal with things.

As Annie approached mid-life she became terrified of relationships. Her past experiences, even back to her childhood, had led her to develop a shield to her emotions.

People in her life had died or left, while others made decisions for her without considering how she felt about anything. People she loved and trusted had abused her and taken advantage of her, or dropped out of her life without explanation.

She left them behind, including a really good man, and their eldest daughter, before they could do it to her, as she believed at the time.

Annie had boyfriends in her teen years, but she always kept her emotional distance.

She had tried to avoid being clingy and almost always succeeded. In her late teens and early twenties, she believed boys would like her if she freely gave herself for kissing, cuddling and ultimately, sex with no ties, unless they wanted them. Annie always let them decide. If they liked her, she clung to them with both hands with no consideration of her own feelings. She didn't really know how she should react and behave. She was just grateful to be liked by someone, especially a boy.

After being single for more than twenty years, Annie sought the closeness of a companion, a close friend, or maybe a lover.

In her early fifties, she met people all the time, at the local RSL club, at work, and on her travels, but none seemed right to her. Then she met a man one evening at the club.

He was travelling on his own. Annie caught his eye and he approached. He bought her a drink and they began to chat. They shared jokes and laughter for the rest of the night and for the rest of his stay in town. Annie couldn't get him out of her mind. He was special.

For almost ten years, they had remained close friends despite the fact they didn't meet for two years or more. They spoke on the phone regularly, and they shared some travels through the outback. They kept in contact wherever they were. This was Annie's dream mate – maybe her soul mate for no other reason, then he was a very close and caring friend.

She met many people over the years, on her travels and through the internet, but they were not her "special friend".

Annie never pushed him to take their relationship to a deeper level. She was almost afraid to be with him full time for fear the bubble might burst. It wasn't ideal, but it was the closest Annie had to unconditional love. The only condition both respected in their relationship was the fact he was still married and shared the majority of his life with a detached wife. She had the house and her life, and he had the shed and his life.

Annie's mate was a real mate but she had to conceal how she really felt about him because he shared his life with a non-participating spouse.

It was always the way for Annie. What she wanted she could never have. What she didn't want or need she seemed to have an over abundance of, especially pain, loneliness and concealed feelings, which she managed to cover up with a positive attitude and her sense of humour.

CHAPTER 17

RELATIONSHIP RELUCTANCE

Annie was afraid of relationships. She was afraid to get too close, to have a one on one connection to that special person as the long-term partner in her life.

Annie found it easier to be mates with blokes and have friendships with other girls. She couldn't trust all her feelings to anyone because, if they hurt her, she'd lose more feelings. She didn't know how many she had left.

All through her life people she loved kept dropping out. Her mother died when she was four, her grand parents who raised her died when she was in her early teens.

There was also the sexual abuse at the hands of her grandfather - very gentle, and in a way, tender, sexual "education". Then there was the bullying, and authoritarian abuse by her grandmother, her dad and an aunty, at different times of her life.

Then other relatives tried to have a hand in "bringing her up", but she never really felt unconditional, unrestricted love.

The man she knew as dad was also distant with his strange, alcohol affected ways, and his bitter, spiteful single-mindedness. He always judged and jumped to conclusions without a parachute. He wasn't really a meaningful part of her life ever. He never asked her about her feelings either. The things he claimed to do for Annie were to appease his own anger and resentment.

Annie was comfortable, well fed and dressed, and everyone made sure she was a "good girl". She did it everyone else's way, no matter where she was living, or who she was living with.

No one ever asked her what she would have liked, or where she'd like to be, or how she felt about anything. No one ever talked to her about her mum. She was always told where to live, where she always had to adapt to the new household and lifestyle - with good manners. She had to do it their way, no matter where she was living.

She had to accept being physically punished by some of them, without question, if they believed she had done wrong. Annie didn't recall ever being given the benefit of the doubt. It was always assumed she did it, whatever it was.

She lived alone after raising her children alone. It was easier. She loved her kids and their children but it was easier to stay out of their way. By keeping her distance, no one could hurt her.

As a teenager, she gave her heart to those who showed her any kindness, attention and closeness, but of course, because of this, she suffered in several ways, including an unwanted pregnancy which resulted in her deciding her baby would be better off is she was adopted.

In middle age she went the opposite way. Older and wiser, she had no intentions of allowing herself to feel too deeply any more. This way, she couldn't get hurt, dumped, abused, bashed or worse. She could keep her head on straight, she didn't have to compromise her feelings or explain herself to anyone.

However, Annie was afraid she was denying herself a chance at real love. Friendship with distance was easy, but that next step of giving someone else just that little bit more, was too risky. She couldn't afford to lose anyone else, or anymore feelings.

How could she get her head around all those fears and apprehensions?

Annie met an internet acquaintance of more than six months, and although she hadn't let her guard down on her feelings, she was willing to give a little more than she normally did. He turned out to be the wrong choice, again.

They'd shared a lot of life's experiences up to then, but he confirmed her doubts, even though she didn't have any real evidence of what was to come. He didn't ask her about much, kept trying to inflict his standards on her, and became confrontational when she challenged him and tried to contribute with her feelings and points of view.

Annie concluded he preferred a mush-brained woman with her legs open. She was too organised, confident and competent for most blokes.

So how does she put all these life experiences behind her and start with a fresh head? How can she repair the damage this treatment caused?

She'd been single longer than she'd been with a partner. Annie hadn't had an offer and couldn't refuse, so she kept finding out why the blokes were single.

"Why do I need a bloke? I can change my own light bulbs, mow the lawn, change tyres and put the rubbish out. I can tow a van forwards - and backwards," she declared to herself.

Annie's life had left her with post traumatic stress disorder and some serious health issues, but she didn't let that stop her from travelling and peacefully living the lifestyle she chose, with her heart ready to be open to an honest friend.

CHAPTER 18

SECRET DREAM

Annie hoped she'd meet "the man of her dreams" eventually.

He'd have to understand where she was coming from. He shouldn't try to impress her with materialistic crap.

She didn't have to brag or embellish the truth. Her experiences and character alone should be enough if anyone was interested in her.

She had spent more than twenty five years without a partner. She also spent a lot of time alone, pondering her past, present and future. What was in store for her?

Annie believed a couple, in an ideal world, should be best friends and not argue and abuse each other. Annie needed someone who would support her emotionally, and respect her needs. She knew she didn't need someone who would do selfish things without considering her and their relationship.

Cuddles felt good to her. She didn't get many as a child. Her family was too busy trying to bring her up to be obedient and hard working. She recalls being told how bad she was, how naughty she was and how lazy she was. Then she'd be punished to make sure she got the message.

Annie was reluctant to approach anyone with her arms open, offering a spontaneous cuddle. Even as a child, the tangible side of love didn't seem to be there.

On his last day on this earth, her dad rebuked her for kissing him on the forehead as she left his hospital bed side. While she no longer respected him, she felt some attachment to this very sick bed-bound man. Maybe it was his vulnerability. He died during the night. She was still being admonished in her mid-fifties.

She'd spent her life trying to prove those people all wrong. So she kept her distance and went on with her life the best way she knew how, without family support.

All Annie remembered was how her closest family members would judge her - even punish her for what they believed was bad behaviour, rather than asking, understanding and supporting her.

Annie sought the company of positive people who accepted her for who she was. She avoided people who were negative influences in her life.

When Annie left the nine-year violent relationship, she packed herself, two kids, the cat and a budgie into her little station wagon. With a suitcase of clothes and linen, they moved on with their lives. Although she feared her former partner and the consequences of her decision to leave, she kept working and the girls went into day care. It was the bravest thing she'd ever done, and one of the hardest.

From then on Annie didn't want to give every emotion to anyone in case the wheels fell off another relationship, or they took advantage of her. It was easier to stay single, detached, defensive, distant, and on her own, rather than to be hurt emotionally and physically again. She kept the barriers up, and it would take a very understanding, loving, compassionate person to earn her trust enough to get those barriers down, and not give her any excuse to put them up or run again.

Annie tried to not let it get to her, but she had trouble trusting anyone who became too close, in case they turned against her. She was afraid they'd only see her bad side and not her good qualities, and then they would punish her again. Annie didn't want anyone to put her down ever again.

She wanted someone who would be strong and support her through whatever life brought with it, and accept and support her for the person she was, with positive reassurance.

Annie couldn't stay if the person who was supposed to be her best friend, turned against her. Sometimes it would take the most minor thing to stir the feelings of fear, insecurity and inadequacy.

So it was easier to be single than in what Annie considered the wrong relationship.

Annie had begun to trust a new acquaintance until they said something quite trivial. It triggered the old fear of false accusations. She recalled how she had been forbidden even punished for defending herself in the past, and on this occasion she also felt she couldn't defend herself against this very trivial, but significant comment.

The trauma she was experiencing became too much to cope with, and it was then the breakdown was diagnosed as post traumatic stress disorder - all the result of an innocent comment from an acquaintance.

Annie wanted to believe she could trust her friend with her most private thoughts, without being judged, but no matter how hard she tried to hang on, the trust was gone.

Her life motto became "Ask Me! And accept the answer. Learn to know me before you judge me."

CHAPTER 19

THE ADULT CHILD

Not many of her family ever took notice of Annie's interests. Since her childhood, after her mother died, no one ever asked her how she felt or what her interests were.

They just told her what to do.

Now they were learning about her. *"It's such a pity it took more than fifty years"*, Annie mused to herself.

As she shared her stories with the gathered relatives, she could see the enlightened interest in their eyes. It was the largest gathering of this side of the family since her dad's funeral.

The afternoon began as a visit to her dad's youngest sister, and before long there were two more aunties, and two uncles sitting around the kitchen table, sipping coffee and tea, and eating home made biscuits.

They asked Annie questions about her travel experiences and plans. One aunty in particular, showed intense interest in Annie's work on the cattle stations in Western Australia's Kimberley Region. It gave Annie a chance to relate stories about her experiences in her usual humorous, descriptive fashion, without the fluent "paddock French". Before long, the smiles turned to laughter as they enjoyed Annie's story telling. She was enjoying the family interest and attention.

They had never seen this side of her, nor had they looked for it. How could they? She was moved from family to family in her early years until her late teens, and then from place to place to live and work.

Annie was in the world on her own. Her family was her three daughters and four grandchildren. She loved them all dearly, but they now had their own lives, and she didn't want to be an interfering mother and grand mother. She became accustomed to doing things on her own. It was her own lifestyle.

A week later, on Sunday afternoon Annie noticed an elderly couple looking for around the caravan park where she was staying.

She asked, "Can I help you?"

When the pair turned toward her she immediately recognised them as an uncle and his wife. They were looking for Annie. They talked quite a while about her life and travels. They had lots of laughs and drank tea. They were also impressed with her caravan "home".

The other aunties and uncles also came to see her at home. One aunty described the van as a "palace", and another remarked at how clean it was.

Annie didn't know what they were expecting to see, but their reactions indicated they were impressed by her standard of living. They were all her dad's brothers and sisters.

Her dad's family still carried the charade as if she were their blood relative. She never knew how they felt toward her, but they seemed to accept her now. They also asked Annie about her hereditary health issues and suggested their probable origin.

"How would I know?" Annie thought. *"I'm not a biological descendant. Why do they keep up the charade?"* *"Don't they know, or are they trying to protect me? They probably don't know that I know,"* she concluded.

Annie wondered if she should speak up, or if she should let sleeping dogs lie. *"I'd feel better if I spoke up,"* she thought, *"but what would it achieve?"*

"We shouldn't speak ill of the dead", she reminded herself. *"Mum and Dad can't defend themselves."*

Annie wondered what her father's brothers felt about the entire situation. What do his sisters feel? They all had very different perspectives and they all had lived very different lifestyles.

Her father's youngest sister spoke out openly, but would his other sister open up?

She thought it would only serve to determine she was not part of the family and, maybe her younger, intellectually disabled sister wasn't either.

Only her mother really knew the answer, and she's been dead for more than fifty years. What a mess! What a family! What or who was Annie?

Where did her mother's family stand in this dilemma? Did it matter?

"I suppose not," Annie concluded.

While it would answer some of the questions in her head, it wouldn't change anything. I will remain a mystery.

Annie felt pride at the time. They were finally accepting her for the person she now was, with no apparent judgement. They may have even felt a little sympathy for her - maybe even some remorse because they hadn't involved themselves in her life a little more, as she was growing up.

Now they were seeing the product of their inaction after such a tragic beginning.

CHAPTER 20

COVERED PAIN

Annie's life continued to be a cover up of experiences of the past.

She didn't know if it was depression which followed her mother's death but, when she felt lonely and alone she would go and hide somewhere and cry until she fell asleep. The adult would be angry at her for going away and hiding when she was found.

No one tried to console her, ask her how she was feeling, or why she went to hide. In hindsight, she was relieved, because, at the time, she didn't understand it herself,

Even how she dealt with her life was a cover up. She continued to cover up most of her emotions by removing herself from society during her worst times.

Her sense of humour developed due to covering up much of what she felt. Better to make light of life than to take it too seriously. It was easier to deal with everything.

Annie suffered severe depression for much of her life, and she managed to cover her suffering from those closest to her. Even her immediate family, including her children, never knew what Annie was really feeling deep inside. There was no way she could tell them.

She would stay away from people, especially her family, when things were at their worst.

At times she was almost reclusive. Staying away from the world, within her cocoon, until the worst had passed.

She'd contemplated suicide only once, when her teenage pregnancy was the cause of her turmoil, and no compassion or understanding was shown to her by any of her family. Her dad found some of the tablets she'd taken in the attempt to escape life.

Annie was thankful her dad made her vomit and took her to the local hospital, to overcome the affect of the tablets.

Ultimately Annie believed she had far too much to live for. If she'd succeeded, she would not have her beautiful family. She couldn't have travelled to see the country. She wouldn't have met all the lovely people and made new friends.

When friends came to visit, Annie became very adept at concealing her depression. She didn't want those closest to her learning how she was really feeling, or what she was suffering deep inside. It would have exposed her vulnerability and weakness. She felt guilty and ashamed for being depressed because she felt she had no right to feel so bad when she had a beautiful family, most of her health and her independence.

She had created the image of a survivor, a struggler, an independent woman who only needed help when she asked for it. When she was offered assistance, Annie would reluctantly yield and accept, only to feel extreme gratitude and obligation, which she felt she would never be able repay.

Travelling was Annie's way of remaining remote. By keeping her distance from everyone who may have been directly affected by the real "Annie", she felt safe and secure. Phone messages and emails kept her in touch with family and friends.

In spite of internal turmoil, she had the happy knack of converting most experiences into a comical situation. She always managed to see the funny side. Even when her

health began to decline, her sense of humour prevailed.

There's nothing wrong with me," she would say, "The doctors' just keep finding stuff".

"I'll keep taking the pills until I shake and rattle when I roll. I take pain pills, vein pills, drain pills and brain pills," she would explain.

When she folded to the pain and anxiety, she would still lighten up the situation by calling herself a "crippled, fat old lady".

Annie always saw the upside of a situation and consoled those around her. "As long as I can put two feet on the floor in the morning, it's a good day and I'm alright", she would say.

At times her back pain was so severe she could barely walk but still she would find something to do which required minimum effort, with less impact. Annie always needed to be busy and productive. No one saw the pain she was in. She had become very adept at hiding her suffering.

After she'd retired because of her health, someone asked Annie what was wrong with her. "You don't look sick or disabled," they said.

When she did give an explanation, Annie cringed at the list of health issues which led to her finally conceding, and admitting she couldn't be a reliable employee anymore.

Annie suffered acute Glaucoma which had been treated with laser surgery twenty years before. She had spinal damage caused by arthritis and disc degeneration. She had a heart murmur caused by a damaged aortic valve, as well as digestion problems and high cholesterol. Hyperparathyroidism threatened to cause weak bones, kidney stones and other problems. Severe hypertension and a critical potassium deficiency caused numerous complications. All of which were treated with medication. Arthritis, carpel tunnel, golf and tennis elbow caused Annie great difficulty when attempting manual tasks. She'd never even played golf or tennis.

She had also suffered injury from umpiring too much Netball. Who'd have thought blowing a whistle while running up and down the side lines would cause painful shin splints? "Excruciating" slightly understated the pain of shin splints.

Most of her conditions were not hereditary, but it haunted Annie to know she was leaving this legacy to her children, and probably her grandchildren.

She still felt compelled to keep busy and keep moving. *"No lying in bed all day for this granny."*

Much of Annie's medical problems were caused by adenomas, benign tumours. Surgery removed a tumor from her adrenal gland, a parathyroid and the pituratory gland. These tumors don't produce symptoms of their own. They are researched when issues are discovered as a result of many tests and scans.

A self check one morning Annie revealed a suspicious lump in her left breast. The investigation discovered a large lump, a stage three cancer. A total mastectomy removed the breast and the problem tumor, and radiotherapy for reassurance, gave Annie peace of mind. A mammogram later proved there was no more problems in the remaining right breast.

Now in her sixties, Annie described herself as a "crippled fat old lady with one tit".

A change of back pain alarmed Annie. Once again medical investigation reassured her there was no cancer, "just arthritis", was the diagnosis.

Annie's children were always on her mind. She was contented to know they were happy in their lives. The daughter she put up of for adoption was also always on her mind, and was always consideredin family matters. An absentee sister to the three girls.

This became a reality when Annie received a letter, explaining the details of the experience when she surrendered her baby girl for adoption.

An agency arranged a meeting for Annie to meet her "baby". It was a little bit emotional, but a very happy reunion. We were both encouraged to write a letter to each other.

Annie wrote a poem :-

"We started your life together

But life took us apart.

Your determination to find me

Revealed we are in each other's hearts.

You have always been in my family

In spirit, if not for real.

Love, joy and elation

Don't really describe how I feel.

To reunite with a long absent child

Has completed a circle of my life.

Uniting my extended family

Is a dream fulfilled, and give me peace."

The daughter who had done all the research to find her birth mother, was a woman filled with love.

She wrote :-

"Throughout my life, I have thought of you. In my heart I have only had love for you, and I have had an understanding that my adoption was a decision made only in the best of interest of both of us.

I have been blessed with a loving family. My parents did their best for me, and I have always felt loved and lucky. For some reason I have become bold enough to begin this journey, and I am so pleased that you have responded to the first letter.

I cannot remember a time in my life that I was not aware I was adopted. I guess from a young age, it was shared with me as appropriate.

We had yearly camping trips with two other families with adopted children. I think the dads all met in Apex Club. I am the eldest of two girls, my younger sister was also adopted.

I grew up in the country as a young child and moved to the city at the age of ten years. I played Netball, was a Girl Guide and learnt some music. I was a bit of an outdoor type girl and have loved the various pet dogs and cats that have been part of my life.

From High School I became a Registered Nurse and I have enjoyed nursing in such a variety of settings. My work is rewarding and has brought many wonderful friendships. I have never thought of doing any other job.

I married the love of my life at age 23 years. My husband is a country boy who is very supportive, and had encouraged me to take this step. We have three kids, now aged 21, 18 and 14 years.

Thank you again for choosing to begin this journey. I look forward to receiving your letter in your time."

Annie and her daughter lived relatively close to each other, and continued to keep in contact.

Gardening became Annie's therapy. She derived great pleasure, relaxation and satisfaction from propagating plants, planting them as part of landscaping projects, and watching them grow. Annie literally hid in the bushes. No one bothered her there. She found designing gardens and installing reticulation was particularly satisfying. After all, water was the lifeblood of her work.

She felt great joy when someone complimented her gardens or asked questions about propagation and cultivation.

Annie believed she'd inherited her garden prowess from her grandmother. Yet, as she grew older, she resented her grandmother and dad for all the charades they'd played with her life.

Writing was her other passion - short stories, long stories and poetry. She wrote her stories from her experiences in real life.

Writing allowed Annie to be her real self and express how she felt.

She didn't hide in her writing. She used it to reveal herself.

There was to be another reveal, which Annie had pondered for about 70 years. She had known who her biological father was since she was 14 years old. He had died by this time. Annie also knew she had two brothers, but didn't know where to look for them, or if they knew of her existence and wanted to be found. A chance conversation with a relative, proved my brothers were a reality.

Ironically, Annie's daughter was nursing a patient who had connections to the family of her bilogical father. She called Annie and asked, "Would you like to meet your brothers?"

Annie's emotions overflowed.

Annie contacted them, and a meeting was arranged. It was emotional and fun, as Annie introduced herself as "the family scandal".

Their first connection over lunch was lots of chat about how things between them came to be, and where they were to that time. The initial lunch was followed by a second time together a few months after the first. The conversation ebbed and flowed to the "back in the day". There was no shyness.

Their connection felt like they just hadn't seen each other for a long time, despite the fact they'd never met. They shared their interests in cars and motor bikes, which felt strange yet very familiar. Annie had always been interested in cars and trucks, and driving.

They learned they all had health issues, and unfortunately the older brother passed away soon after, when his body couldn't take any more.

The funeral was a time to meet nieces and nephews and their families. Annie was welcomed with open arms.

She was invited to another family event a few weeks later.

Annie was feeling included, part of the family. She hadn't had this connection with her childhood family for many years. In fact Annie felt abandoned, once again.

Despite losing her mother at an early age, and losing her grandparents in her teens, Annie's family was now complete.

CHAPTER 21

NO MORE

Annie had grown from the childhood shrinking violet to a strong, confident, capable woman.

As a child and young adult, she didn't have enough confidence to speak up for herself. As a mature person she spoke her mind and was not prepared to take crap from anyone.

As a child she was conditioned and trained to speak only when she was spoken to, to be seen and not heard, and to respect all elders, whether they deserved it or not.

Her grandmother's lessons lived long in Annie - long after her grandmother died, and long into her adult life.

She'd been well-trained to be a respectful child, but no one "deprogrammed" her to be an adult. No one would have been aware she needed deprogramming. Maybe the family she grew up with left it to Annie's dad, but he would never have given it a thought. In fact, he never seemed to give her much thought at all, except when he believed she'd done something wrong.

Annie's dad was too wrapped up in his own world and lifestyle. He believed he could judge her and think the worst of her without defense. She had to adjust and blend in. She always had to adjust and blend in. No one did it for her, or was she being too selfish to expect it?

When did she stop being a child? When would she be allowed to speak her mind as a person in her own right? When do other people stop being respected elders and become equal adults?

There had been no one around to give Annie the go-ahead to be an adult.

She didn't want to stop the respect, just the distinction between her adult self and other adults.

In adulthood being submissive and compliant were not useful qualities in the world of self-preservation.

It wasn't until she was out in the big, bad world, alone with her young children, did she find the strength - and herself.

Those who now knew her did not know of her highly disciplined childhood.

There was no one to support her or help her pick up the pieces of her life, but there were plenty willing to judge her rather than accept her.

"Anyway, while they're putting shit on me, they're getting dirt under their fingernails", she resolved.

When she started out on her own again, Annie found a nail file and kitchen knife were her best friends when it came to repairs around the house. There were not many household break downs which couldn't be fixed using these "tools" - even filing the distributor points and cleaning the spark plugs in her car.

Annie didn't have to pick her battles, they was thrust upon her, like her battles with the Government support agency over eligibility to benefits.

The agency had accused her of neglecting to report her income correctly, and it claimed to have overpaid her as a consequence. The agency was now claiming more than a thousand dollars overpayment and demanded Annie repay it over time, by deducting it from her fortnightly payment. Her determination and insistence on keeping records stood her in good stead.

Annie's tight record keeping also helped her plead her case, resulting in the agency actually owing her eighteen hundred dollars. This was the first of numerous battles with this Government agency over many years.

After her house burnt down, she was allocated a brand new public housing residence. It was a lovely three-bedroom house, which Annie worked very hard to make a home. This brand new house had bare concrete floors, and no garden.

Annie made some enquiries with the state housing office to determine what they did to assist new tenants settle in. They admitted they provided vinyl floor coverings to the kitchen and passage, if the tenant wanted it.

Annie had accepted an offer of a friend to lay straw matting in the lounge room. She placed mats at the front and back doors. So when she learned about the vinyl flooring she accepted with both hands.

She treated the high-quality, neutral-toned floor covering with several coats of floor polish which served to protect the surface, and made it easier to clean.

There was no top soil around the yard. When the site was cleared and leveled for building, the soil and any vegetation was removed. Annie also learned the state housing office could supply twenty tonnes of top soil. She took it.

A friend was driving tip trucks carting soil to some road works in the region. He offered to bring in another twenty tonnes of top soil, so she could make a garden.

When she initially moved into the new house another friend presented her with about a dozen seedlings of native trees and shrubs as a house-warming present. Now all she had to do was spread the forty tonnes of top soil, plan the layout and plant them.

She spent the next week spreading the soil from the pile in the front yard around and across the back and front yard, with a bucket and a borrowed wheelbarrow. She had no neighbours yet in the newly developed cul-de-sac, so she borrowed equipment from the builders.

She seconded another friend's utility to get some grass runners from the sand dunes along the foreshore. Annie spent the next two weeks planting and nurturing salt water cooch runners which would eventually be the lawn.

She then went out to another friend's farm and found mallee tree logs. The logs were all cut to two metre lengths to make them easier to handle. Then she placed them along the front of what would be the garden beds around the fenceline, as a retaining edge, and back-filled the beds with some of the new soil.

Annie then did the landscaping, planting the seedlings in the most appropriate places to create shade, shelter, and living privacy screens. She also created a vegetable garden in the best corner of the site where it would received the most sunshine and shelter from the wind.

After four years the property looked a picture, and Annie surveyed her patch with pride. The children enjoyed the open spaces and the swing set she'd erected.

Her strength and independence gave her the courage to study journalism, gain a diploma, and work as a news correspondent with the national radio network from home.

As a journalist, Annie also learnt to come forward. She met and interviewed people from many walks of life, including celebrities, sports stars, politicians and prominent people in the community.

The work required Annie to attend numerous meetings and court hearings, talk to prominent members of the community, and investigate and report on matters of interest to the wider community, including major crimes. She successfully contributed freelance work for more than ten years.

The success of her business depended on her wits alone. Annie used her initiative to find the story and the subject of the story, conduct interviews, write the story and read the news on the local radio station's morning bulletins.

Only confidence in her own skills led to her success. She was able to support her family on the income derived only by her skills with the written word.

When asked how she entered the journalism field, she simply replied, "I had a mid-life crisis and became a journalist." She had to find, write and read the news, turning a hobby into an industry.

Annie developed enough confidence in herself to undertake travel and jobs along the way, which were totally foreign to her as a young adult.

She had never been allowed to express herself to the families she spent her childhood with. She was now able to hold her own and use the freedom of writing to express herself and tell other people's stories.

It took many years of ups and downs, and physical abuse for Annie to develop any sort of personality of her own.

She had no idea who she really was in her younger years. She just went along with everyone. She was even punished for expressing her own feelings in her second long-term relationship.

Asking for love and respect resulted in tears and bruises. So she learnt to keep her head down and her mouth shut in any later relationships. Annie found it easier to go it alone.

She went on to nurture her own character to be an organised, confident, middle-aged woman. She joined groups and volunteered for management and committee duties for community, emergency services and sporting organisations.

This did not go down very well with a few of the men she met along the way. She concluded they came from the chauvinistic world from which she'd escaped. Annie declared she would eventually recover from any experiences with male chauvinists who, she considered were unfortunate experiences in trousers.

She moved on and purchased a caravan to travel and live in. Annie loved caravan travel and park life.

It was with this large caravan and four wheel drive she set out to travel around Australia.

Alone, but not lonely, Annie traversed the highways, hills and bends of the nation's roads with her favourite music in the tape deck, and the voices on the UHF-CB radio for company.

Annie was confident enough to tow, negotiate traffic and road trains. She had a great deal of respect for the nation's truck drivers whom she believed carted the country's wealth on their wheels.

Hearing their opinions shared over the two way radio, really opened her ears, and her eyes, to the plight of the truckie. This was especially evident during the time of extremely high fuel prices.

Annie pulled into caravan parks and roadhouses, and, with guidance, reversed her rig into the allocated sites. She loved the social contact. Even her chronic health conditions couldn't stop her.

Annie would tell anyone who asked, "As long as I can get up the caravan steps, and in and out of the car, I'll keep travelling".

She'd become an extremely independent person, and only when necessary did she ask for help. Not that she was foolish. She didn't want to be a nuisance, an imposition, or obliged to anyone, so she lived away from her children.

So she lived life alone, and she sometimes covered the loneliness. Annie was prepared to live this way, rather than to sacrifice her independence, or to be dominated by anyone who couldn't respect her as an independent equal. She continued to be the victim of commitment phobia.

By avoiding close relationships she avoided being hurt once again.

CHAPTER 22

SELFISH GUILT

More than fifty years after her mother died, Annie became overcome with guilt again. She had never considered how her mother's death impacted on other peoples' lives.

At the age of four Annie was oblivious to the family circumstances, and nobody had explained what was happening. No one asked her how she felt, or what she wanted.

She was simply told, "Mummy died".

She had all those unexplained feelings and unanswered questions about her life after her mother died. She never thought about anyone else who was affected by the death. Annie judged herself very harshly.

She had made mistakes during her life, and guilt over these mistakes was the cause of much of her anxiety.

Now, fifty years later, Annie was feeling very guilty. She never gave a thought about how anyone else felt at the time. She didn't consider her grandparents - her mother's parents, her dad - her mother's husband, nor her mother's two brothers, and their families.

Her dad's youngest sister was one of her mother's best friends. About fifty years later she told Annie how shocked she was at the time, and how much she missed her friend for a long time after her death. This aunt revealed that Annie's mother had confided in her about her life and her third pregnancy.

Through an unfortunate chain of events, Annie's mother left a lot of devastated, sad and lonely people behind.

Annie's grandmother was a dominant, matriarchal woman who controlled much of her family's affairs. Annie's mother, the only daughter, was also the subject of the control and dominance.

At the age of twenty, Annie's mother became pregnant to a married man.

The illegitimate, unwanted pregnancy had to be covered up from relatives and friends.

The illegal sexuality of a close male friend also had to be covered up. A marriage of convenience was arranged.

Annie's mother was locked into an unsatisfactory marriage which could not have been fulfilling physically or emotionally, despite the couple sharing a bed. Annie could remember jumping on her parent's bed sometimes.

A second child was conceived and born while Annie's mother was in this unfulfilling marriage. The baby girl was born with severe intellectual disabilities. The man Annie knew as "dad" wasn't the father of the second, disabled child.

There was a third pregnancy. This time Annie's mother was overcome with guilt and attempted to abort the foetus, with the assistance of her doctor and medication.

The drug-induced termination resulted in haemorrhage which caused double pneumonia, and ultimately ended the young woman's life. Annie's mother was just twenty five years old.

Annie's dad never forgave his mother-in-law or the doctor who treated his wife. He remained bitter until his death, more than fifty years later.

How could a child of four years old comprehend these things?

Throughout her teenage years and all the turmoil thrust upon her by well meaning, or not so well-meaning adults at the time, Annie could only follow their "instructions" on how to live and behave. How to or not to miss her mother wasn't one of them.

The impact of Annie's mother's absence became more evident when she became a mother and a grandmother. The older she was, the more she missed her mother. Annie often reflected on what could have been, had her mother lived. What could have been?

Those events exposed her feelings of guilt, and how selfish she had been to resent the actions of the family and their efforts to protect her from the world.

Annie felt guilty for not comprehending what her mother must have gone through, but she had never blamed her for leaving her and her sister.

It was more than fifty years later when Annie learned of some of the real facts surrounding her mother's death, beyond the family's protective version.

Although Annie had felt resentment towards her dad as the truth about his lifestyle was revealed, she never felt any guilt about how she felt about him. The man Annie knew as "dad" was gay.

Annie concluded her dad was an angry, spiteful man, mostly towards his former mother in law.

When Annie left the home they shared, this man burnt and destroyed all her childhood keepsakes.

She did feel some guilt over not considering how he must have felt or how he dealt with his personal turmoil at the time, and into the future. They never discussed it.

CHAPTER 23

PERCEPTION OR DECEPTION

Annie was raised in a narrow minded, judgmental Christian society, where it appeared high-profile good deeds were to leave an unforgettable legacy of nobility to the church and wider community.

The judgmental, unchristian actions and words of her grandmother went through to the keeper. "Do as I say, without question". Annie often referred to herself as a "genetic Lutheran".

She believed her grandmother's philosophy may have been, "I do as I do. Then society may overlook my matriarchal control over the family, relatives and friends, and the sad consequences."

Annie was also confused about the contradiction of the Ten Commandments.

She interpreted the philosophy as, "Love your neighbour as long as he wasn't Catholic, Presbyterian, Methodist or a member of other churches, or go to the public school.

As Annie grew up, she woke up. This was simply not right!

She even learned that she couldn't catch any non-Christian diseases, or curses from the other churches and faiths. They were nice people too.

Annie also learned all people were relatively equal, no matter what their bank balance, life style, faith and social standing was. You wouldn't go to hell if the hat, bag and shoes didn't quite compliment the outfit worn to church.

"Maybe", Annie reasoned, "If nana covered up the misdeeds of her only, adored daughter and a married man, the community would overlook this because she was such a fine, upstanding, benevolent, charitable person. If she arranged a marriage between her only adored, pregnant daughter ,and her homosexual friend, it would avert any attempt of the law and society from condemning them. She would be forgiven because she meant everyone well, with no malice or judgment."

Did this family matriarch take any responsibility for her only, adored daughter's sudden, untimely, premature death?

Did this matriarch feel an obligation to raise the first child of her adored daughter?

Now Annie had to console herself with the belief her grandparents took her in as an admirable, noble gesture, out of the goodness of their hearts, rather than for unconditional family love.

Or was she being too harsh?

Despite all the false starts and unhappy times, Annie wasn't bitter or resentful. In fact, she believed she was lucky.

Annie believed she was lucky to have had a good family care for her, without suffering too many battle scars, mental or physical. In fact she was content knowing she had survived life's lessons as a stronger character with a quick and cheeky sense of humour.

She believed everyone needed a laugh, and her favourite advice to her friends and acquaintances was, "Ya gotta have a laugh!"

Whatever the reason, Annie became her own person, with her own character, spirit and family, in spite of it, or because of it.

You decide.

In her later teen years, Annie felt popular, and enjoyed the company of new friends. Annie believed sex was the way to get and hold friends.

As a result Annie became pregnant.

She was judged, but had no family support. The black sheep featured again. She felt so desperate, and at this stage in her life, Annie failed at a suicide attempt

After six months in a "unmarried mothers home" Annie gave birth to a beautiful baby girl. She made the decision early in the pregnancy to put the baby up for adoption.

With no support, no where to live, not job, she faced the future alone. It proved to be a necessary, but heartbreaking decisision. The baby girl would have a better chance at a better life with a loving family.

THE END